PORTFOLIO / PENGUIN

THE GOOGLE GUYS

Richard L. Brandt is an award-winning journalist who has written about Silicon Valley for two decades, including fourteen years as a technology correspondent for *BusinessWeek*. He is also a consultant to entrepreneurial companies. The author of the blog *Entrepreneur Watch* and the book *Capital Instincts*, he lives in San Francisco.

The Google Guys

Inside the Brilliant Minds of Google Founders
LARRY PAGE and **SERGEY BRIN**

Richard L. Brandt

Portfolio/Penguin

Previously published as *Inside Larry and Sergey's Brain*

PORTFOLIO / PENGUIN
Published by the Penguin Group
Penguin Group (USA) Inc., 375 Hudson Street, New York, New York 10014, U.S.A. ●
Penguin Group (Canada), 90 Eglinton Avenue East, Suite 700, Toronto, Ontario, Canada
M4P 2Y3 (a division of Pearson Penguin Canada Inc.) ● Penguin Books Ltd, 80 Strand,
London WC2R 0RL, England ● Penguin Ireland, 25 St. Stephen's Green, Dublin 2, Ireland
(a division of Penguin Books Ltd) ● Penguin Books Australia Ltd, 250 Camberwell Road,
Camberwell, Victoria 3124, Australia (a division of Pearson Australia Group Pty Ltd) ●
Penguin Books India Pvt Ltd, 11 Community Centre, Panchsheel Park, New Delhi–110 017,
India ● Penguin Group (NZ), 67 Apollo Drive, Rosedale, Auckland 0632, New Zealand
(a division of Pearson New Zealand Ltd) ● Penguin Books (South Africa) (Pty) Ltd,
24 Sturdee Avenue, Rosebank, Johannesburg 2196, South Africa

Penguin Books Ltd, Registered Offices:
80 Strand, London WC2R 0RL, England

First published in the United States of America as *Inside Larry and Sergey's Brain* by
Portfolio, a member of Penguin Group (USA) Inc. 2009
This paperback edition with a new afterword published 2011

10 9 8 7 6

Copyright © Richard L. Brandt, 2009, 2011
All rights reserved

THE LIBRARY OF CONGRESS HAS CATALOGED THE HARDCOVER EDITION AS FOLLOWS:

Brandt, Richard L.
Inside Larry and Sergey's brain / Richard L. Brandt.
p. cm.
Includes bibliographical references and index.
ISBN 978-1-59184-276-7 (hc.)
ISBN 978-1-59184-412-9 (pbk.)
1. Google (Firm)   2. Page, Larry, 1973–   3. Brin, Sergey, 1973–   4. Internet
industry—United States.   I. Title.
HD9696.8.U64G6634 2009
338.7' 6102504—dc22   2009012967

Printed in the United States of America
Set in Vendetta with Catull and Myriad Pro
Designed by Daniel Lagin

Acknowledgments

Thanks to Kim and Leila Brandt for their patience and support over my preoccupation with this book, which took substantial time away from them. Also, Shel Israel for helping me get started; my agent, Al Zuckerman, who has supported me far beyond the level I had any right to expect; and my editor, Jeffrey Krames, for taking a chance on me and doing so much to support me. In addition, Mark Powelson provided me with substantial research, and Kim Girard and Andrea Orr helped out enormously with early original reporting in 2004, several years before this book came together in its current form. Finally, thanks to everyone at the Progressive Grounds Café in San Francisco, where most of this book was written, for keeping me supplied with great lattes.

Contents

The
Google
Guys

Introduction

The World's Librarians

Good luck. I've been trying to do that for some years.

> —Google CEO Eric Schmidt after being told the title of
> this book

The world's first great library was the Great Library of Alexandria. It was created by Ptolemy I, a childhood friend of Alexander the Great and a general in his army. Ptolemy inherited rule of Egypt—which the army had conquered—after Alexander's death in 323 B.C. Ptolemy made the small, backwater town at the mouth of the Nile, named after the great conqueror, his new capital. By creating the library, somewhere around 300 B.C., he turned his city into a thriving center of intellectual thought envied by the world. It reigned as the greatest library in the world for three hundred years.

Ptolemy's goal was to collect all the written works in the world and put them in one place. By the time the library was destroyed, it was said to contain more than five hundred thousand papyrus scrolls, collected over three hundred years. The library played a critical role in the Hellenistic Age, the period during which Greek culture spread into much of civilized Europe, Africa, and Asia. Probably no other library has had such influence on cultures and knowledge—until the great library of the Internet was created more than two thousand years later.

The Internet's librarians sit today in a tidy campuslike business complex in Mountain View, California, the epicenter of Silicon Valley. It's a campus of modern steel, concrete, and glass structures interlaced with trees, gardens, walkways, and artificial ponds and streams, where people travel by bicycle, by scooter, and on foot among—or inside—the buildings. These librarians are a universe away from the gray-haired ladies with glasses dangling from chains around their necks and an incredible knowledge of the Dewey decimal system of many childhood memories. This, after all, is the electronics age.

Google Inc., a thriving corporation teeming with youthful and smart computer scientists and an incredible knowledge of the Internet, has become the de facto head librarian of the world's information; the entity that guides us through the labyrinthine web of online information, philosophy, entertainment, opinion, debate, slander, pornography, art, and worthless blather that the geeks and executives of the Internet like to lump into the single category of "content."

Larry Page and Sergey Brin did not create the Internet

(although they now employ one of its key architects, Vint Cerf). But if anybody embodies the soul of the world's head librarian, it's the brainy pair of Larry and Sergey. They created the heart of Google's philosophy, its business tactics, and the ethos behind all major issues—from censorship to user privacy to entering new markets and trying to change the business tactics of existing corporations.

Google Is Ethical

They're unlikely business moguls. Larry is the more socially awkward of the pair. Heavily eyebrowed, thick-lipped, with a perpetual five o'clock shadow and conservatively cut black hair always in need of a comb, he rarely volunteers to answer questions unless specifically asked to address them. When he does, it's with a methodical intonation that sounds like a baritone version of Kermit the Frog. Sergey is also shy with outsiders, but more poised, with a piercing stare and curly brown hair piled on top of his head as though it's unable to settle down. They work together on all major company decisions, from ethical issues to product design, usually in meetings that can be brutally taxing. But Larry, as president of Products, is the primary thinker about the company's future direction, and weighs in heavily on key hiring decisions. Sergey, a mathematical wizard and president of Technology, is the arbiter of Google's technological approach and shows deep interest in the company's moral stance.

Facing questions from shareholders and the press at a recent corporate annual meeting, Larry sat stiffly in his chair, straight-backed in a blue dress shirt and brown slacks, his hands on his knees, one of them holding a microphone as if he didn't know quite what to do with it. Sergey was more relaxed in a brown T-shirt and faded jeans. He sat comfortably with his forearms resting on his legs, looking over the crowd with an air of intelligent and confident interest, more willing to address sensitive topics than one would expect from such an intensely private entrepreneur.

At this meeting, Amnesty International had presented two proposals, demanding that shareholders require the company to set up a human rights committee to examine its practices in China, with the aim of limiting censorship there. Management felt that this was already being done, and rejected the proposal. But in a show of solidarity with those who have concerns about the issue, Sergey decided to abstain from voting his shares, neither agreeing nor disagreeing with it. True, it was a largely empty gesture, since the board and management had plenty of votes to reject it, but he wanted to demonstrate an acknowledgment of the difficulty of the issue. Larry and CEO Eric Schmidt voted against the proposal.

I asked Sergey why he abstained, and he explained that he was sympathetic to the cause and agreed with the proposals in spirit. "Directionally, the two proposals are correct," he said. "I think there is certainly room for us to have a group of independent people in Google who meet regularly to discuss these questions," he said. But he also said he was proud of Google's actions in China, where he felt the company's record was better than that of its competitors.

Google Uses New Business Tactics

It's just one of many issues that have focused the spotlight on Google's ethical stance since the company was founded in late 1998 by these two Stanford University computer science graduate students. Google came out of a project that only a computer scientist could love: developing technology to search through large electronic databases of published research papers. Instead, they came upon a much greater solution—a better way to search through the giant morass of data that is the Internet—and ended up turning their technology into one of the biggest, most influential companies in technology today.

But technology alone does not make a successful company. Business tactics do. Larry and Sergey have created a unique company with a new kind of business model, employing tactics that fit the Internet Age like Alexandria's Great Library fit the Hellenistic Age. Google may not last three hundred years, but it still has a huge future in which its influence will continue to grow.

To say Larry and Sergey struck the right business chord would be the understatement of the twenty-first century. When they launched Google, they were entering a war that pundits were insisting they had already lost before they even got started. In mid-1998, it was Yahoo Inc. that sat on top of the World Wide Web. Yahoo had become one of the premiere Internet sites, the place where 75 percent of Web searches were begun. More than twenty-five million people visited Yahoo every month. In September 1998, it became one of the first pure Internet companies to claim a profit.

The previous March, *Fortune* magazine had summed up the prevalent view: "Yahoo! has won the search-engine wars and is poised for much bigger things," its editors declared. Its stock was soaring past $100 per share, on its way to a peak of $230 at the end of 1999.

Then it all fell apart. By mid-2000, Yahoo's stock was in free fall, on its way to hitting the bottom at under $5 a share. Yahoo CEO Tim Koogle, once hailed as a great Internet visionary, was a year from being fired. Nobody seemed to know what hit them. Whatever it was, it missed Google.

What happened was that the world changed. Before December 31, 1999, Y2K paranoia was scaring corporations worldwide into pouring billions of dollars into new computers and software. Technology companies were growing fat, and their stock prices were growing fatter. A robust market for technology stocks inspired venture capitalists to pour money into dot-com companies and take them public on nothing but a business plan and a prayer. Day traders followed their lead and bid up the dot-com stocks. The stock market was soaring so high that the Federal Reserve tried to cool irrational exuberance by raising interest rates.

Every one of those moves turned out to be wrong. On January 1, the Y2K panic proved to be unfounded and the money tap that fed Silicon Valley was shut off. All at once, corporations stopped buying computers. Profits at technology companies plunged, their stock prices were sucked down with their declining earnings, and high interest rates made it worse. The unprofitable dot-com companies saw their stock prices drop to pennies a share, and venture capitalists (VCs) stopped investing. The real Y2K disaster turned out not to be crashing computers, but a crashing Internet market, triggered by the end of the Y2K fear-induced spending.

Google Stands Out

But there was one standout. As the cash flow that had kept the technology world afloat reversed direction, Google seemed to catch the runoff. In January of 1999, the Google search engine was handling ten thousand search queries a day. A year later, this had grown to ten million per day. Google took in revenues of $200,000 in 1999. In 2000, the start of the technology recession, its sales grew by 940 percent, to $19 million. By the end of 2002, when most dot-com companies were either desperately dehydrated or dead, Google's revenues had bloated to $440 million. In 2003, just four years old, its sales hit $1.5 billion, its profit was $100 million, and it had taken over some 80 percent of the world's search queries.

Why Google? It turned out the VCs were right about one thing. The Internet had created a huge change in businesses. But in this time of tectonic economic shift, most dot-com companies were still playing by the old rules. They didn't notice the flaws in their strategy because they were being kept afloat by the billions of dollars from venture capitalists and day traders pouring into the industry. Larry and Sergey not only went with the flow of change, they also accelerated the pace.

Larry and Sergey figured out the new rules of business, piece by piece, driven by an overwhelming motivation to build a great company. They put together a business model for the Internet Age. They tinkered with different ways to make money and hit on the most profitable form of advertising anyone had ever seen. Big advertisers were doing their usual recessionary retreat, but Google focused on small advertisers looking for bargains. With no substantial competitors in either search or online advertising, Larry and Sergey arguably created an Internet advertising monopoly on a par with Microsoft's domination of the PC software business. For better or worse—and it's mostly better—Google has become the new Microsoft, while Microsoft is becoming the old IBM, overtaken by a new technology.

Google now employs about twenty thousand people, but just two of them set the pace and guide its evolution. Larry and Sergey work together like two halves of a well-balanced machine. CEO Eric Schmidt is responsible for growing revenues, but the decisions that Larry and Sergey make are the fuel that powers that revenue growth. Everybody in the company refers to them by their first names—sometimes as the single unit Larryand-Sergey—but treats them like emperors, the final arbiters of all important decisions.

A young, smart, and athletic kid whose family escaped the oppression of the communist Soviet Union and a clever young geek from Michigan with a fondness for Legos would seem a very unlikely pair to create a business revolution. Asked by reporter John Ince in 2000 what Google's biggest challenges were, Sergey admitted it was learning to run a business. "The most difficult part has been learning to deal with organizational challenges. We have over 70 people now. It's a more complicated beast. It's not very clear how to keep everybody productive and focused. That's been more of a learning process. Business dealings . . . have been a little bit new to us."[1] But they've turned Google into more than just a great company. They almost single-handedly revived Internet businesses and changed the rules of commerce on the Internet.

Contrary to popular belief, Google's success was not simply a matter of inventing a better mousetrap and watching the money flow through the door. The initial design of Google's search engine did not have technology much more advanced than its competitors. It was how they used and refused to abuse the technology that mattered. Larry and Sergey have been successful because they have completely rethought the process of catching mice. Not surprisingly, they're upsetting a lot of business fat cats in the process.

Their business model is completely transforming modern industries, including computer hardware and software, telecommunications, publishing, broadcasting, and entertainment. It is changing cultures and political systems. They have commercialized the Internet and started an Information Revolution the way Thomas Edison spurred the Industrial Revolution by harnessing electricity and saying, "Let there be lightbulbs."

But revolutions do not come easily. They arrive like an invading army, pillaging industries in their path. One group's revolutionary is another's corporate terrorist. Google's fans see it as a corporate version of Thomas Jefferson, or a freedom fighter trying to spring dissidents from a Gulag work farm. Its enemies think of it more like Joseph Stalin, and are mobilizing to attack Google like capitalist idealists fighting the Red Menace. Competitors, Hollywood executives, book publishers, copyright holders, privacy advocates, civil rights activists, and government regulators are menaced by Google's Leonid Brezhnev–like secrecy and enormous power.

Google Has Unique Strengths

Google has two enormous strengths, neither of which is appreciated with nearly the awe it deserves. They have little to do with software, and almost everything to do with an Internet-dominated culture and unparalleled computer power, both homegrown.

Google's success made it inevitable that it would become the most controversial company that does not currently have top executives facing criminal prosecution over creative accounting practices. Google's view of what's evil and what is not gets it into a lot of trouble.

Much of the ire directed at Google is due to corporate resistance to the massive changes Google is thrusting upon the business world. Established companies, accustomed to a century of doing business in a certain way, are understandably confused by the rapid changes, and afraid of them. Google is the obvious target of anyone trying to stem the inevitable sea change in business. In the long run, fighting that change is akin to building a sandbar to try to hold back the coming tide. But that doesn't stop them from trying.

Larry and Sergey are wickedly clever. They break the mold. They challenge old industries and make a lot of enemies. They're ruthless businessmen. Most of all, they're idealists, believers in the power of the Internet to make the world a better place.

They have a lot of fans and have been thrust onto the world stage. Larry and Sergey have become friends with Al Gore, Richard Branson, and San Francisco mayor Gavin Newsom, and they're huge fans of Barack Obama. Mayor Newsom is one of the people greatly impressed with Larry and Sergey and what they've accomplished. "Google is a phenomenon the likes of which you rarely see in a lifetime," he told me recently. "I just love these guys. They feel a profound responsibility to deliver great things because they're capable of it. They want to have a life worth living. That's what's made them such a phenomenal success today."

They're not infallible, and they're not saints. They make mistakes and happily drive competitors out of business. They have, at different times, irritated their investors, their CEO, Wall Street, and business partners. Competitors say they have created a monopoly, with all the power and danger that this brings. That problem is exacerbated by the fact that they operate with almost paranoid secrecy, and have mostly retreated from the public spotlight. They rarely give interviews and have an almost mystically enigmatic reputation second only to that of Steve Jobs. Unlike Jobs, however, they're shy and awkward around non-geeks. Almost everybody who knows them well works for them. Says Robert Davis, the former CEO of onetime search company Lycos, "I've never met them. Can you imagine that? They're about the only people in this industry that I haven't met."

Larry and Sergey *are* Google. Aside from their recent marriages, Google is their life. But even in marriage they didn't stray far from Google. Larry married Lucy Southworth, a biomedical informatics doctoral student at Stanford who has done medical work in South Africa and "wants to better the world." (They tied the knot in December 2007 at Richard Branson's estate on Necker Island in the Caribbean.) Sergey married Anne Wojcicki, a biotech analyst whose company, 23andMe, Google has invested in. (Their May 2007 ceremony was conducted on a sandbar in the Bahamas to which guests either had to swim or take a boat to reach.)[2] Anne's sister, Susan, is a Google executive and the person who rented out her garage to Larry and Sergey to help them get started.

Google's stinginess with information has become a running joke among journalists. When the *San Francisco Chronicle* informed Google it was going to report on Sergey's marriage before the fact, spokespeople warned the paper's executive vice president, Phil Bronstein, that it would damage the paper's relationship with the company. His response was "What relationship?"

Google Sometimes Looks Evil

The problem is that a secretive company looks like a company with something to hide. The intrinsic mystery surrounding Google, and the founders in particular, is a huge problem, probably the biggest for a company that relies heavily on the trust of the people who use its products. Google must be trusted to protect the astounding amount of data it collects about people who use its services—from hackers, from spammers, and from government spies. Many people wonder if Google isn't evil after all.

Google does not fit the profile of other companies we might consider evil. It has not been involved in any stock scandals. None of its executives has been forced to do the perp walk in front of TV cameras. It has not been accused of back-dating stock options. It has never been accused of fudging its financial statements.

Increasingly, Larry and Sergey find that their ideals, their dedication to the free dissemination of any information they can get their computers on, is landing them in court. Seven years ago, Google had one lawyer on staff. Now it has more than a hundred. At a shareholder meeting a few years ago, one stock owner stood at the microphone and asked, "What are you being sued for these days?" David Drummond, Google's head attorney, responded, "How much time do you have?"

The question that seems to be on most people's minds these days is whether Google is becoming an evil corporation. Certainly competitors, copyright holders, and others think so, because

Google is infringing on their revenue base. Privacy advocates think so, simply by virtue of the fact that Google holds an incredible amount of data about individuals.

In the end, it's tough for anyone to trust a company so big, so powerful, and in control of so much personal data about nearly everyone. One accidental security breach resulting in hackers' obtaining personal data from Google's archives—the most likely scenario of breaching the public's trust—would be devastating to Google's reputation. The question of whether Larry and Sergey can be trusted with all that data can never really be answered in the affirmative. But one mistake can answer it in the negative forevermore.

Larry and Sergey are in the position of Gary Hart, would-be presidential candidate in the 1980s who brazenly challenged reporters to find any scandals about him. The press promptly complied by catching him in an extramarital affair, thus ending his presidential aspirations.

In the case of "Don't be evil" Google, it's the bloggers who have set out to prove, in any esoteric way they can, that Google is becoming evil as it gets bigger. Most of the arguments are along the line that money and power corrupt, so Google is corrupt. As Google collects more information about individuals, it becomes Big Brother. These concerns may be real. But the arguments are overwhelmingly "what if?" scenarios, rather than actual examples of evil.

The latest culprit is the Web browser that Google launched in 2008, after saying for years that it was not interested in that market. But Larry and Sergey changed their minds, and people see this as a duplicitous change.

Clint Boulton, who writes the "Google Watch" blog for eWeek, asserts that the simple fact that Google is entering Microsoft's territory makes it evil by default. "It's hard to be the overwhelming leader in search and not be considered a monopolist, which in business is code for 'evil,' " he writes. And, he adds, "It's impossible to be that powerhouse, then launch a Web browser to serve as the gateway to your Web services and not be considered blackly evil."[3] Boulton argues in a later blog that as a company becomes big, it needs more revenues to feed its machine and, as everybody knows, "more money equals corruption."[4]

The situation was exacerbated when the online site Valleywag actually read the onerous nondisclosure agreement that came with Chrome, Google's new browser. It stated that any content that people "submit, post or display" when using Chrome automatically gives Google "perpetual, irrevocable, worldwide, royalty-free, and non-exclusive license to reproduce, adapt, modify, translate, publish, publicly perform, publicly display and distribute" the information.[5]

It turned out that this was one of Google's standard nondisclosure agreements, which slipped past without Google's management noticing. Google quickly retracted it, replacing the agreement with the explanation "In order to keep things simple for our users, we try to use the same set of legal terms (our Universal Terms of Service) for many of our products. Sometimes, as in the case of Google Chrome, this means that the legal terms for a specific product may include terms that don't apply well to the use of that product."[6]

But Google uses a very similar agreement when guest lecturers give talks at the company, a regular occurrence. San Francisco psychiatrist Thomas Lewis felt he was giving away the rights to his research in order to give an invited talk. When he complained, he was told to list beforehand everything he was going to talk about that he had the rights to, and it would be excluded. His lawyer told him to make the list huge, and wouldn't mind if he came as close as possible to including everything in the world. He did so and gave his speech.

Or try Matt Asay, who writes The Open Road blog for CNET. Google has a group of applications that people can download for free, called the Google Pack. These programs are a mix of software from Google and third parties. Before Chrome, Google included the open-source Firefox browser as the default browser in the pack. After Chrome, it still offers Firefox as a choice, but now Chrome is the default choice. That move, Asay says, "has Google looking more like the old Microsoft monopoly it replaces."[7]

But, of course, it's Google's entry into China that gets the main criticism. In order to enter that market, by law it has to agree to censor the results of its own search engine. One alternative is to stay out of China completely, as a protest against censorship, which many Google critics insist would be the right thing to do. The other is to run a Chinese-language search engine offshore without censoring it, which would mean that access to the site would be cut off from China by the Chinese government anytime something came up that the officials didn't like. And, in fact, Google does run just such an offshore search engine, in addition to the one based in China. It just doesn't get much traffic.

Google executives have idealistic excuses for entering China, based mainly on the theory that some information serves the Chinese population better than none. That's a fine argument, except that there are several other search engines operating in China to fill the gap (all of which also censor themselves), including China's homegrown Baidu. All Google can claim to do is push the envelope as much as possible to free up information. Nevertheless, the decision to enter China is the one that nags most at the founders' consciences—especially Sergey's.

But Larry and Sergey are growing up, maturing with the company they command, learning to compromise and to mellow the mercurial pursuit of their idealism that dominated Google's early days. And they're going to be around for a long time. They've tackled the beast of business, and won.

They've also been lucky, and their rise has seemed almost effortless from the outside. But luck is insufficient fertilizer for growing a business as successful and dynamic as Google. There's brilliant method in the founders' madness. As usual, the angel is in the details.

Chapter 1

Arbiters of Cyberspace

Human salvation lies in the hands of the creatively maladjusted.

—Martin Luther King, Jr.

Ptolemy I was a childhood friend of Alexander's. Born in Macedonia, a Greek-speaking region at Greece's northern border, they arrived at the peak of Macedonia's power. The Greeks, however, considered Macedonians to be barbarians, and refused, for example, to allow them to join in the Olympic games. Alexander's father, King Philip II of Macedonia, changed the status quo by conquering the Greek city-states and uniting them under one country. Although a ruthless conqueror, Philip instilled in his son a dedication to Greek culture. As a youth, Alexander studied under Aristotle, who taught him philosophy, science, medicine, rhetoric, and literature. Philip's goal, passed on to Alexander, was to spread the enlightenment of Greek culture to the rest of the world. His friend Ptolemy, who studied with him and was a historian and a poet, was the one who accomplished this by creating his library at Alexandria. Alexander and Ptolemy were conquerors, but they were also idealists, trying to spread Greek learning, literature, art, and science throughout the world.

L arry and Sergey's families came from just beyond the outskirts of the status quo. Before either of them was born, their families crossed that border into academic life. They lacked the wealth, the connections to the business elite, and the capitalist instincts that Bill Gates showed when he was still in high school. But neither did they rise from extreme poverty as did Andy Grove, the CEO of Intel who drove the company to great heights after arriving in the United States as a young, brilliant, and penniless Hungarian refugee with a bulldog determination to thrive.

Larry and Sergey came from highly intellectual families that had faced more than their share of battles against powerful institutions. Larry's family waged labor union battles against the American auto industry, while Sergey's family suffered through government oppression and discrimination in the Soviet Union.

The Leftist

Larry has more in common with left-wing documentary filmmaker Michael Moore than with Microsoft founder William H.

Gates. Larry's family had working-class roots in the General Motors company town of Flint, Michigan, the hometown of Moore portrayed in his film *Roger and Me*.

Larry's grandfather was an autoworker and a politically leftist member of the Teamsters during its antagonistic battles with the youthful auto industry. The union was led by factions with communist influence. Larry's grandfather participated in possibly the greatest labor struggle of the early twentieth century, the Flint Sit-Down Strike of 1937, when the workers took over a major auto factory. Larry still keeps a memento from those days: a hammer that his grandfather carried with him for protection during the acrimonious strike.

But Larry's father, Carl, broke out of that environment and became a leading computer scientist, a talent his sons inherited. Born in 1938, Carl Page survived childhood polio, which left him somewhat fragile throughout his life. He was also the first person in the family to graduate from high school (in 1956). He then went on to the University of Michigan to study engineering. While still an undergraduate in 1959, Carl Page was hired to work in the university's Logic of Computers Group, a pioneering research team headed by legendary computer scientists such as Art Burks and John Holland. He earned two bachelor of science degrees in engineering in 1960, one of them in the specialty field of computer science—the first graduate with a degree in that field at the University of Michigan. In 1965, he earned his Ph.D. in computer science from the same university.

The sixties was the time of Sputnik and the race to the moon, when good computer scientists were in demand from the aerospace industry, but Carl decided to remain in academia. After graduating, he had a short stint teaching at the University of North Carolina, but returned to Michigan (where Larry was born in 1973) and joined the faculty of Michigan State University in 1967. Although MSU did not have the prestige of the University of Michigan, Carl was a talented pioneer in computer artificial intelligence. He was also a visiting scholar at Stanford University in the 1974/75 academic year, and spent a year as a researcher at NASA's Ames Research Center in Mountain View, California, in 1978.

Most of the Page family is scientifically and academically oriented. Larry's mother, Gloria W. Page, taught computer programming at Michigan State. (His parents were later divorced.) He has an older brother, Carl, Jr., who served as his entrepreneurial role model. After earning a master of science degree at the University of Michigan, Carl, Jr., went on to become cofounder of a dot-com company called eGroups, which was sold to Yahoo in the summer of 2000 for $432 million in stock. Larry's younger sister, Beverly, still lives in Michigan. Sadly, their father, Carl, Sr., died of pneumonia in 1996, just as Larry was starting the research to create Google. The loss affected him deeply.

The Tinkerer

Coming from such a computer-literate family, Larry Page naturally developed an early fondness for computers. In 1979, when he was six, his family obtained a very early home computer called the Exidy Sorcerer. His brother wrote an operating system for the machine, not long before a young company called Microsoft began modifying an operating system for the first IBM PC. With the help of a homemade typing program and a dot-matrix printer, Larry used the computer as a word processor to complete an assignment for a school class. It was the first time anyone at the school had ever seen something produced on a word processor—or heard of such a thing.

Larry attended a Montessori school early on, and thrived in its self-paced learning environment. His parents encouraged his curiosity and love of tinkering. When Larry was nine, his brother gave him a set of screwdrivers, and he immediately set to work dismantling every power tool around the house he could get his hands on. The popular account is that his parents were less than thrilled because he couldn't put them back together again.

It's an event that Larry laughs about today. When I ran into him at Google recently, I asked him if the story was true. He looked up and smiled. It wasn't that he couldn't put the tools back together, he said. "I just didn't."

That's believable, because he has always been more likely to build things than tear them apart. He got his undergraduate degree in engineering at the University of Michigan in 1995, winning many honors, including the university's first Outstanding Student Award. But he's fonder of telling people how he built a working programmable plotter and inkjet printer in a casing he made out of Lego blocks while at the University of Michigan. He also started showing his entrepreneurial interest at Michigan, taking business classes and joining the LeaderShape program, which teaches its members the skills to be leaders in society.

When he entered the Ph.D. program in computer science at Stanford, he arrived with a strong foundation both in computer science and in liberal politics. As with many academic families, Larry's had never lost its leftist roots, and remained politically active. When his father died, the family requested that friends give donations to the Democratic Party rather than buying flowers. That political bias dominates Larry's personality—and that of Google as well. More than 90 percent of political donations by Google employees today go to the Democratic Party, and employees overwhelmingly supported Barack Obama over John McCain in 2008. CEO Eric Schmidt campaigned for Barack Obama and served as one of his economic advisers. Schmidt, Larry, and three other Google executives donated $25,000 each to fund a $150,000 party at Obama's inauguration.

The Refusenik

If Larry Page carried the hammer of his family's past, Sergey (or Sergei) Brin carried the sickle. He was born in Moscow, also in 1973, when it was still the seat of power of the old Soviet Union.

Both Larry and Sergey are Jewish, but that ethnicity has affected Sergey's family more than it has Larry's. Sergey's father, Mikhail (changed to Michael when he came to the United States) Brin, was a curmudgeonly intellectual and a gifted mathematician. At first he wanted to study physics at Moscow State University and become an astronomer. But he was turned down because the Communist Party banned Jews from the physics department; the government didn't want them to have access to Soviet nuclear secrets. So he decided to study mathematics instead, and took the entrance exams in rooms reserved for Jewish students, appallingly nicknamed the "gas chambers."[1] Mikhail graduated with distinction in 1970. Sergey was born three years later.

Considering the Soviet hunger to prove its technological superiority over the United States in the 1970s, a talented mathematician would normally have been recruited into the space program or military research. But this choice was not offered to Mikhail Brin. He wanted to continue his studies at the university, but was turned down, again because of the anti-Semitism prevalent in the USSR.

Without a graduate degree, he settled for a meaningless job at Gosplan, the Russian economic policy planning agency. His Orwellian task was to come up with the right statistics to demonstrate that the standard of living in the Soviet Union was higher than that of the United States. He hated the job, but it was better than being shoved off to some research station in Siberia. His wife, Eugenia, also managed to endure the anti-Semitism and got a degree in mathematics; she later worked in a research lab at the Soviet gas and oil institute.

In his spare time, Mikhail continued his studies in mathematics, and managed to publish papers in respected math journals. He probably would have had an easier time getting a Ph.D. in economics, but he obviously did not have much love of Soviet-style economics and was more interested in an academic career. He convinced two lecturers to be his advisers for a doctorate in mathematics, submitted his thesis to Kharkov National University in the Ukraine, a backwater compared to Moscow, and earned his Ph.D. in 1975. "He pursued his work against great odds," says Anatoly Katok, a longtime friend and colleague from Moscow. "There was resistance from the establishment. They didn't want Jews and they didn't want outsiders."

In 1977, Mikhail attended an international conference, where he met foreign researchers and academics. It was a life-changing event. He went home that night and told his wife that they had to get out of the country and settle in America, where real opportunities lay. The problem was that just expressing a desire to leave the Soviet Union put them in danger of being declared "refuseniks," which would have caused even more discrimination.

But the one advantage Russian Jews had at that time was that they were among the few who were allowed to emigrate from the Soviet Union. Katok, also a mathematician suffering from the same ethnic advantage as Brin, had developed connections at the University of Maryland, and with their sponsorship, he managed to emigrate first, in 1978, and secured a teaching position at the university. He then worked to help his friend Brin find a position there as well.

In 1978, Brin's family applied for an emigration permit, one that included Mikhail's mother. They told the authorities that they wanted to settle in Israel, which is what many Jewish emigrants from the Soviet Union did. But applying for emigration got Mikhail fired from his job; Eugenia had to quit hers, and the family had to relinquish its Soviet citizenship. While they were waiting for their application to be reviewed, Mikhail earned money translating technical documents from English to Russian. Without jobs, they struggled for several months, but in 1979 their application was approved—just in time. Soon afterward, the Soviet government ended all emigration.

Leaving almost all their possessions behind, the Brin family set up temporary residence in Paris, often the first stop from Moscow. Some families end up as refugees, stranded in a country for months or years until they manage to obtain a visa to their new country. But Katok and other colleagues helped Mikhail (now Michael) secure a visa and a teaching position at the University of Maryland.

"Both myself and Michael Brin were fortunate because there was tremendous empathy and solidarity from our colleagues," says Katok. "We were able to avoid being refugees in the usual sense."

Sergey didn't know the extent of the anti-Semitism his parents faced until much later in life. But it affected him nevertheless; he has said that even as a child he never felt at home in Russia. Although the family was never deeply religious, Sergey has visited Israel three times, the first time as a teenager with his family. While there in 2008, he gave a rare interview to *Ha'aretz* magazine, and confirmed that the difficulties his family had experienced in Russia "certainly had a significant effect on my life subsequently." He noted, "My family had a lot of challenges in the Soviet Union. . . . I think that just kind of gave me a different perspective in life."[2]

The Brins had very little when they reached the United States. Sergey told *Ha'aretz*: "The U.S. was very good to us. It was a great place, but we started with nothing. We were poor. . . . When we first moved to the States we rented a little house, and my parents didn't have a proper room to sleep in. They had to wall off the kitchen. It was a very humble beginning."

What role did this play in molding his character as an entrepreneur? "We learned to get by," Sergey said. "I think being scrappy and getting by is important. . . . The most important thing is the background [of being Jewish]—of just having gone through hardship and being able to survive and thrive. I think that's at the core of the Jewish experience." But he never went through the process of having a Bar Mitzvah at age thirteen. "At least in the U.S., bar mitzvahs are associated with getting lots of gifts and money, and I was never comfortable with that."

The Math Prodigy

The family did thrive, although not nearly to the extent Sergey has. Michael Brin is now a mathematics professor at the University of Maryland. His mother—over sixty when the family emigrated—taught Russian for several years at the University of Maryland. Eugenia became a scientist at NASA. Sergey was six years old when his family landed in Maryland. His brother, Sam, was born in Maryland in 1988.

The elder Brin is still a curmudgeonly and short-tempered man, although, says Kenneth Berg, a fellow professor at the University of Maryland, "There is not a ruthless bone in his body." But he was a tough professor, gruff enough to hand graded papers back with the comment "My sincere condolences." He's also a stern parent. "Michael has always been very demanding and judgmental," says Katok. "Sergey was certainly very bright, but kind of quiet. His dad had exacting standards and I don't think at an early age he really appreciated the brilliance of his son."

Michael Brin discovered his son's promise one day when Sergey was eight or nine years old. Katok and other colleagues from the university were sitting around the Brin house listening to Michael complain about how stupid his undergrads were. He had tried giving them a graduate-level math problem, just a little above the capabilities of most undergrads, he grumbled, yet not one of the students had had the brains to solve it.

Sergey, who had been quietly sitting in the corner, decided to speak up, and in his "squeaky little voice," according to Katok, offered a solution to the problem. At first, his father dismissed him. Katok then interjected: "No, Michael. That's the correct answer." Adds Katok: "In my memory, it was the first time Michael took his son seriously."

Sergey was also fascinated with computers at an early age. He got his first computer, a Commodore 64, around 1982, when he was nine years old. He soon discovered the Internet. For a while, he frequented primitive chat rooms, then called IRCs, or Internet relay chats, but later recalled that he grew bored with them once they became dominated by "10-year-old boys trying to talk about sex."[3] He, on the other hand, was a ten-year-old boy interested in computer games, and graduated to multi-user dungeons (MUDs) where computer whiz kids stayed up late to battle each other as virtual warriors. He even wrote his own MUD game.

Like Larry, Sergey also attended a Montessori school until about age ten, and was quite happy there. But he was bored with high school and dropped out after three years. There was simply nothing left for him to learn there. His father started calling him the "high-school dropout." Instead, however, he applied to the University of Maryland and was accepted a year earlier than the average high-school graduate. He was taking senior-level mathematics classes after about a year, and took several graduate-level courses before he graduated. He also took summer jobs at prestigious research labs at Wolfram Research, General Electric Information Services, and the University of Maryland Institute for Advanced Computer Studies.

Around 1993, he downloaded an early version of Mosaic, the graphical interface that evolved into the Netscape browser and turned the esoteric Internet into the point-and-click World Wide Web, leading millions of people online. "I thought it was pretty cool," he said in January 2000. "It was a fun thing to play with."[4]

Kenneth Berg, from whom Sergey took a differential equations course at the University of Maryland, knew he was a very promising mathematician. Berg recalls writing on the board a geometrical proof of a problem when Sergey politely raised his hand and explained, from a purely conceptual level, why that proof could not possibly be true. Berg looked at the board and realized he had written down the proof incorrectly.

"It was really impressive," Berg says. "He really understood how to think mathematically from a very young age." Even then, adds Berg, Sergey offered his opinion without arrogance. "He simply saw something wrong" and felt the need to correct it, says Berg. Still, no one today would accuse Sergey of any lack in the ego department. He always had a tendency to correct teachers, professors, and colleagues, and retains that habit today.

Still, Berg adds, "He's a super nice guy. There's a gentle spirit about him. He seems to be somebody who wants to use his intellect to do good."

Sergey graduated in 1993 with a dual degree in math and computer science, and entered the Ph.D. program at Stanford in 1994. He had turned out to be such a brilliant mathematician that his father expected big things from him. But business mogul was not one of them. After Google was started, Michael Brin told the University of Maryland student newspaper, "I expected him to get his Ph.D. and become somebody, maybe a professor."

Dr. Larry Brilliant, who is now chief philanthropy evangelist at Google.org, the company's philanthropic arm, believes that both Larry's and Sergey's family backgrounds are what make them idealists with a tendency to favor small corporations and individuals over the business elite. "Inside their minds, what's at the core of Larry and Sergey—and they'll disagree on this, so it's not like it's an absolute—but they come from a very moral base," he says.

"Sergey was raised in the Soviet Union and his family went through a hell of a lot. He doesn't ever want to see that happen again. He approaches things not necessarily looking at them from the top of the food chain. He's much more sympathetic to regular people."

There's no denying Sergey's brilliance. In fact, when he joined the Ph.D. program at Stanford, he passed all his qualifying exams in the first couple of months after arriving. Most students don't pass all the exams until their third year. That meant he didn't actually have to take any classes—just write a thesis in order to get the degree (which he never did). "Sergey didn't have to take the Ph.D. program seriously," says Scott Hassan, a grad student at Stanford who worked with him (and later went on to cofound his own company, eGroups, now part of Yahoo).

But Sergey Brin is not simply a pasty geek with no life outside his math and his computers. He's an athlete with many interests: dancing, sailing, gymnastics. He trained on the trapeze as a youth and once said he seriously considered running off to join the circus. He's physically fit and known to walk around on his hands for the fun of it (and to impress women).

He's a competitive swimmer, and when he first entered the graduate program at Stanford, his father groused that he "majored in swimming." Michael Brin has claimed that the only course Sergey ever took at Stanford that required him to write a paper was one on computer cryptology. When he asked his son if he was planning on taking any advanced classes, Sergey reportedly answered he was "thinking about advanced swimming." His father didn't know about Sergey's fondness for skinny-dipping with friends or picking locks to office doors in the old Economics Building at Stanford. "He's a phenomenal lock pick," says Brian Lent, a former Stanford colleague. But Lent insists they never did anything illegal, such as entering the dean's office to change grades. But they thought about it.

As smart, precocious boys with access to education and technology in the 1980s, both Sergey and Larry became very early users of the Internet, absorbing its culture, the world of Dungeons & Dragons and MUDs, and the free software on offer.

The Shire

Sergey and Larry are the hobbits of the Shire of the Internet. Although they were born a generation after Steve Wozniak, Apple Computer's cofounder and the original technology hobbit, they were more like him than like Steve Jobs or most of the Bubble generation of Internet entrepreneurs.

Internet technologists are comfortably rooted in their personal shire of science and technology and academe, leagues away from the turmoil of the modern business world. Many of them have day jobs. They're prone to being easy-going pranksters with a fondness for a good online party with others like them. In 2001, when the first *Lord of the Rings* movie was released, Larry and Sergey rented out an entire theater and took the Google staff to see it.

They grew up in an environment that encouraged open programming, and they shared their creations freely in the academic tradition. What college student doesn't appreciate free beer, music, games, programs, and information to get them through the next exam? The Internet provides everything but the beer.

Larry not only used Legos to build a computer printer in grade school, he repeated the stunt when he built Google's first computer server at Stanford. However, he did not actually use Legos at Stanford, but rather knockoffs of larger blocks called Duplos. "They're imitation Duplos, because they were cheaper than the real thing," Sergey once explained. "This turned out to be a big mistake, because the tolerances [the deviations in the way the parts fit together] on the imitation Duplos are much worse than the tolerances on real Duplos, and as a result our system would crash from time to time, because these things would fall apart and the whole disc array would go down and you couldn't do any searches."[5] (The device is now on display in the Gates engineering building at Stanford.)

Even today, Sergey and Larry—especially Larry—are still shy when outside the circle of other technologists. In person, they don't generate that air of superiority so common in Silicon Valley CEOs. They even seem deferential. Still, having succeeded so effectively in school and as entrepreneurs, they developed the luxury of rarely dealing with outsiders, a trait that many people see as arrogant and dismissive—which it often is.

When Larry and Sergey met at Stanford and started working together, they found they shared not only a profound love of computers, but also a strong left-wing bias and a devil-may-care attitude. They distrusted business moguls.

This is true also of the rest of the technology elite who helped build the Internet. The original designers of the Internet never intended it to reach out and touch anyone beyond the domain of the universities and government labs for which it was created. These groups used the Internet to share their research, ideas, and software programs—all for free. Most of them are advocates of the Open Source movement, which believes technology standards should be built not on patented, corporate-owned software, but on generally agreed-upon technology available to anyone. They contributed technology to the Internet's growth as well. In the 1980s, the Internet started quietly growing in capability right alongside the much noisier personal computer industry.

But a funny thing happened on the way to the 1990s. Since anyone sufficiently technical could tap into the Internet with their own computer, it was soon co-opted by groups of invaders its builders never envisioned. The true Internet pioneers were hackers, online game players, software pirates, and independent programmers who wanted to share their creations with the world. The Open Source advocates soon came to power.

But Larry and Sergey have now ventured beyond the truly dedicated Open Source movement by creating a corporate giant. And for that, most of the Internet purists have labeled them as evil. Blog postings from the tech elite complain that the pair has created a dangerous monopoly, a huge corporation that is taking over the Internet, filing patents and exploiting the Internet for profit.

Larry and Sergey still dominate Google. One or both of them—usually Larry—still interviews major candidates for employment, particularly those in engineering. They are rabidly dedicated to Google, and promote its mission—to organize and make available all the world's information—with the zeal of evangelical cultists. And they're willing to take on anyone, or any company, that stands in their way.

Chapter 2

Accidental Entrepreneurs

Eighty percent of success is showing up.

—Woody Allen

When Ptolemy created his library, he encountered problems nobody had faced before. The biggest was that no one had ever tried to organize such a massive collection of scrolls so that people could find what they wanted. It's difficult to locate the text you want among half a million papyrus scrolls stacked randomly on shelves. The *Republic* by any other name just ain't the same as Plato's.

That's where the great librarians of Alexandria stepped in. The first librarian of the Alexandria library was a man named Zenodotus. He struck upon the most enduring classification system ever dreamed up by humankind. He alphabetized the scrolls of Alexandria. In short, a simple concept that we now take for granted was not dreamed up until the Library of Alexandria made it necessary, five hundred years after the Greeks developed their alphabet. As the library grew, even that system was not sufficient. Callimachus, a poet and scholar believed to be the second or third librarian, created the first bibliography. He divided the documents into several classes—rhetoric, law, epic, tragedy, comedy, lyric poetry, history, medicine, mathematics, natural science, and miscellanea—in a document called the *Pinakes ton en pase paideia dialampsanton kai hon synegrapsan* ("List of those who distinguished themselves in all branches of learning, and their writings"). The Pinakes alone was said to have taken up some 120 scrolls. It was probably never completed, and did not survive to modern times. But for generations it was the major source of research for scholars, and it became the model for bibliographies in the millennia since.

And the innovations just kept coming. A poet named Philotas wrote the first comprehensive dictionary at the library, which Zenodotus improved by alphabetizing it. Didymus wrote commentaries and glossaries of the works. Dionysius Thrax created the first book on grammar, which became the standard text on Greek grammar for a thousand years and influenced the Roman creation of Latin grammars. The concepts dreamed up two millennia ago in Alexandria are still used today.

I n their early days at Stanford, Larry and Sergey did not plan to make their search engine the core of whatever company they started. They viewed it as a scholarly research project, new technology that could find just the right documents in the giant library of the Internet.

In 1997, while still graduate students working on Ph.D.s in computer science at Stanford, they showed great enthusiasm when discussing their creation. One person they enjoyed chatting with was Andrei Broder, a corporate researcher at a Silicon Valley company called Systems Research Center, where he led the team that created the hottest search engine of the time, AltaVista. Broder, a Stanford alumnus, used to visit the campus to see what interesting projects were in the works. Two of the bright graduate students he would occasionally chat with over coffee were Larry and Sergey.

Broder found them to be "obviously very intelligent, and out to reinvent the world." But when the discussion turned to the topic of making money from the technology, Broder found that Page had a profound difference of philosophy on the subject. "It was a very funny thing about Larry," Broder recalls. "He was very adamant about search engines not being owned by commercial entities. He said it should all be done by a nonprofit. I guess Larry has changed his mind about that."

Brian Lent agrees with that view. He worked with Larry and Sergey on their search engine project for a while, until deciding to head off and join a start-up. (He's now CEO of Medio Systems Inc., which sells search and advertising systems for mobile phone makers.) The problem with the Google search engine at the time, Lent recalls, is that Larry and Sergey didn't want to commercialize it, and Lent was anxious to become an entrepreneur. Their mantra at the time was more socialistic than entrepreneurial. "Originally, 'Don't be evil' was 'Don't go commercial,'" says Lent.

That view was more Larry's than Sergey's. While at Stanford, Sergey wrote a scholarly paper about their creation, titled "The Anatomy of a Large-Scale Hypertextual Web Search Engine." Still, in that paper, he argued against an ad-supported service as a corrupting influence. "Advertising-funded search engines will be inherently biased towards the advertisers and away from the needs of the consumers," he wrote.

But contrary to many reports, the two weren't against corporations per se. Any graduate student who applies to Stanford, the genesis of Silicon Valley, is keenly aware that it's a great place from which to launch a company. Larry and Sergey just didn't expect Google to be the fountain that would quench their thirst to be entrepreneurs. They felt that a search engine was too important to be corrupted by financial interests.

Craig Silverstein, another computer science Ph.D. candidate at Stanford, helped get the company started as employee number one. He was the one who didn't really want to start a company. But, he recalls, Larry and Sergey did. "Larry always wanted to be an entrepreneur," says Silverstein. "He always thought big about what the company would be. Sergey was a good partner for that. He thought the same way." Silverstein ended up putting his academic career on hold in order to join Google, where he still works.

Finding Hidden Meaning

Larry stumbled his way into creating a search engine almost by chance, pushed by two different forces—a government-funded research project and the rise of the Internet. Their work was funded by a project called the Digital Library Initiative, which started as an attempt by the Department of Defense to make it easier to find computer research papers electronically.

DLI originally had nothing to do with the Internet, which in 1994 was not yet a major force in the digital world. Stanford's original grant proposal to DLI that year didn't even mention the Internet.

But in 1994, Netscape Communications released its graphical Web browser, and the following year, the world suddenly had a system to archive and share anything, making DLI redundant. It was also the year that Yahoo Inc. was started. "The Internet completely changed things underneath us," said Professor Hector Garcia-Molina, chair of Stanford's Computer Science Department at the time.[1]

Whenever a new technology comes along, few people really figure out how to exploit it properly. Generally, it's the second generation of companies that makes the real advances. That was true for search engines. Throughout the 1990s, search engines primarily retrieved pages according to how many times given key words were found on a site. These engines didn't take advantage of the interconnected properties of the Internet other than that they could find sites and archive their information. The new technology that the Internet demanded did not yet exist. Larry created it.

When Google's search engine was officially launched in December 1998, it was distinguished by one big unique attribute: it worked.

At its core is the PageRank system, invented by Larry (and named after him) while he was working on his Ph.D. It takes advantage of the unique properties of the Web—the network of links that makes its name so apt.

Garcia-Molina recalls how it all started. He was Page's adviser, and one day in 1995 his student came into his office to show him a neat trick he had discovered. The AltaVista search engine not only collected key words from sites, but could also show what other sites linked to them. AltaVista did not exploit this link information in the way Google would, but that day in Garcia-Molina's office, Page suggested it would be a good way to rank the importance of sites.

At first, it was just a game. "We had lots of fun that day seeing which computer science pages were most popular among the different universities," recalls Garcia-Molina. They were pleased to find that Stanford's database group, for example, drew more links than a similar department at rival University of Wisconsin.

Larry had his own idea about links. He told Garcia-Molina, "If this is so important to us, why not make it part of the search process?"

Larry's idea was inspired by his scientific background. It was well known in the scientific community that when a researcher cites your paper in his own, it lends yours more credibility. The more citations you get, the more important your paper is perceived by the research community. This idea was codified in the "Science Citation Index" created in 1960 by Eugene Garfield, founder of the Institute for Scientific Information. Larry reasoned that Web links were analogous to scientific citations, and those with the most links probably were the most popular and would prove most useful to searchers. Those were the sites that should be listed first in the search results. He then began creating his own software for analyzing links between sites.

This required some tricky programming. Not only did the system count links to a particular site, it went a step further by determining the importance of the sites doing the linking. This was done by counting the links to the sites one link back. This increased the complexity of the analysis enormously; in order to calculate relevance, PageRank also had to track the links two steps back and correlate that data with the key words. Larry first called the system BackRub, because of its property of tracing links backward. But he later settled on the more sophisticated PageRank, a double entendre with his surname.

Sergey also fell into search engine research by chance. As a math and computer science major in the doctoral program at Stanford, he was working on a research project within the database group. In 1995, he and Brian Lent decided to try their minds on another computer science discipline called "associative data mining." This is the process of finding pieces of information that commonly occur together. Retailers use it to search through their sales records and determine whether different items are frequently bought together by customers. Data mining was, however, a new field for computer science. It required archiving masses of Web data, so Sergey had to write a "crawler" program—software that visits Web sites, summarizes their content, and stores the data in a central location accessible to graduate students and search companies. Other search engines already had their own crawlers.

Sergey is a terrific programmer and engineer. His data mining work, using the Internet, involved parsing through huge amounts of data. "He did it on a scale that others would not have even contemplated," says Jeffrey Ullman, Sergey's adviser. (Sergey's paper outlining the Google search engine was itself cited in another scientific paper, "Quality of Service and the Electronic Newspaper: The Etel Solution.")[2]

Sergey is also a clever hardware engineer. He needed disk drives to store the data he collected, but had very little money, so he bought the cheapest drives he could find. But when he tried them out, they weren't fast enough. Instead of throwing them out, he figured out a way to make them work anyway, by doubling the number of terminals on the drive connections. "I had never thought of doing that," says Ullman. "This was engineering of the first order."

Their separate projects brought Larry and Sergey together in late 1995. "I was chatting with Larry a lot," recalls Sergey. "He and I got along pretty well."[3] If Larry wanted to search the Web, he also needed a crawler. So he recruited Sergey to the Digital Libraries project, combining his search technology with Sergey's Web crawler.

They made a great combination. "Sergey likes math things," says Stanford professor Andreas Paepcke, who headed the Digital Libraries project. "Larry just wanted to build. It just kind of grew."

Scott Hassan, another Stanford grad student who worked with Larry and Sergey, recalls that it was mainly Larry's project. "For Larry, it was his primary thing. Sergey was just doing it because it was interesting to him." They generally worked late into the night on indexing and parsing Web pages at a Fresh Choice restaurant in Palo Alto, which offered a "Student's Special" buffet for five dollars. They often toiled until 5:00 A.M.

There Will Never Be Another Yahoo

At Stanford, Larry and Sergey's search engine could analyze thirty to fifty pages a second. Two years later, that rose to about a thousand a second. Today, it's millions. It took a lot of research and programming to make it work. "We developed a lot of math to solve that problem," Sergey told an interviewer in 2000. "We convert the entire Web into a big equation with several hundred million variables."[4]

They played around with different names for their search engine. One of them was the "What Box." "But then we decided that sounded like wet box, which sounded like some kind of porn site," Sergey recalled.[5] Looking for a big number, they intended to call the crawler Googol—a word coined by the nine-year-old nephew of mathematician Edward Kasner for the number 10^{100}. Kasner simply wanted to name the biggest number anyone had ever given a name. He then also coined another name, the Googolplex, which is ten to the power of googol. (Larry and Sergey later adopted the name GooglePlex for their corporate campus.)

Nobody thought this would be the basis of a new company. Most people thought that Yahoo had already won the search engine wars, although Yahoo was really a classification system akin to the Dewey decimal system (without the decimals). It was a portal and did not even have its own search engine, licensing one from Akamai instead. The other search company executives didn't think that search technology could or needed to be improved. Larry knew differently. If the Internet was to reach its potential, it needed new inventions to make it easier to find the right stuff. Without Google, the Internet might still be in the pre-Hellenistic Age. Nevertheless, Lent says, "In early 1996, we all said, 'There will never be another Yahoo.'"

Just because this was an academic exercise, it didn't mean Larry wasn't ambitious. In order to build a system to test their theory, he and Sergey were repeatedly borrowing money from other students and faculty, and "borrowing" equipment that arrived at the loading dock at Gates Hall before its owners could claim it. "We had stolen all these computers from all over the [computer science] department," recalled Sergey.[6] Finally, Professor Garcia-Molina asked Larry exactly how much of the Internet he wanted to search. Larry's response: "All of it." Garcia-Molina managed to get them some money from the Digital Libraries project so they could buy more computers.

The Google search engine, first set up to troll through Stanford's own Web pages, was an immediate hit with students and faculty, and Page and Brin became convinced of its commercial potential. By late 1996, Sergey recalled in an interview, "We had something we thought was quite nice."[7]

Who Wants a Search Engine?

But they still didn't think this would be the basis for a company. They planned to finish their Ph.D.s, so they tried to sell their technology to other search engines.

Fortunately, they found no takers. Had they succeeded, Google would not exist. For one thing, Larry and Sergey were pricing their technology very high, at about $1 million.

Most companies turned them down flat. Around 1997, for example, Larry called Louis Monier, one of the creators of the AltaVista search engine at Digital Equipment Corp. (DEC). AltaVista was then considered the best search engine in existence. "He tried to explain to me who he was and what he was doing," Monier recalls. "He sounded interesting. He didn't sound like a crackpot or anything. I said, 'Yeah, we should meet.'"

But DEC management showed no interest. The company was not really interested in a search business; AltaVista had been created mainly to demonstrate how its computer server "was bigger and beefier" than other hardware, says Monier.

Before Monier could talk to Larry and Sergey, he needed permission from DEC headquarters in Massachusetts. But now that Google had commercial potential, Larry's obsession with secrecy emerged. He insisted that Monier sign a nondisclosure agreement first, and DEC management wouldn't go for that. "This went nowhere, which was too bad," says Monier.

Finding Funding

It seems today that it was always inevitable that Larry and Sergey would turn their search engine into a company. But that was not the case. "Larry has a million ideas," says his early partner Craig Silverstein. "If he didn't make a company out of this, he'd be happy to make it out of something else later. If they had found someone who took their work seriously, and wanted to own it and offered the right price, they would have sold. We didn't find that, so we said, 'Okay, we'll do it ourselves.' " In 1998 they began looking for investors to get them started.

They approached David Cheriton, a computer science professor who had started a couple of companies with Silicon Valley entrepreneur Andy Bechtolsheim, for help finding funding. He decided to introduce them to Bechtolsheim. Just taking the step of asking Bechtolsheim for money was a bold and brash move. They had no business plan or formal pitch. Luckily, Bechtolsheim didn't need either. According to Sergey, he simply said, "Oh, we could discuss a number of issues. Why don't I just write you a check?"[8] He filled out check number 4642 to Google Inc. for $100,000.

In the end, Cheriton matched Bechtolsheim's investment, and with those two on board, the rest of the start-up money they needed came easily. Technology angels and executives, such as Ron Conway of the Band of Angels and Ram Shriram from Amazon, also put in money.

Those who did invest made fortunes. Stanford, which holds the patent to the PageRank algorithm Larry created, received 1.8 million shares of Google stock in exchange for long-term rights to the patent. Stanford's profit was $336 million, by far the most money it has ever received from spinning off technology invented on campus. It's probably the most money *any* university has ever received from a single invention. Cheriton, already wealthy when he became the second investor in Google, is now a billionaire. One Stanford professor who loaned Larry and Sergey money when they were students joked that the stock he received in return would cover his retirement.

But this initial funding could get them only so far. So in the spring of 1999, Larry and Sergey started seeking $25 million in venture capital. Again, they were incredibly brash. For the money, they were willing to hand over less than one fifth of the company's equity—thus valuing the company at more than $125 million. Most Silicon Valley companies have a hard time getting that much money, and they give away a much larger percentage of the start-up's ownership to get it.

But the fact that they had already persuaded Bechtolsheim and other prominent angels to invest impressed enough people to allow Larry and Sergey to get the pick of the litter. They went to the top of the heap, and got interest from two of the most prominent venture capital firms, Kleiner Perkins Caufield and Byers, and Sequoia Capital. These firms are used to setting their own terms, and most entrepreneurs feel lucky if they can even get in the door to make a pitch. But Larry and Sergey did not want to give too much control of their company to any individual firm, and insisted that they split the deal: each venture capital firm could invest $12.5 million in return for 9 percent of the company.

It almost killed the deal. Both firms wanted to do the investment alone. John Doerr from KPCB and Mike Moritz from Sequoia had never come across entrepreneurs refusing to take their money before. Just having one of them on board lent extraordinary credibility to any entrepreneur trying to make a name for himself.

Finally, Larry and Sergey went to two of their angel investors, Ron Conway and Ram Shriram, and said they wanted to drop out of the deal and seek more angel funding instead. They told the angels that they were giving the firms only a couple more days to decide.[9] Conway and Shriram had a good relationship with each other and were sometimes coinvestors with Doerr and Moritz, and they passed the threat on. Faced with the prospect of losing any part of the deal, both Doerr and Moritz caved. With this deal, Larry and Sergey showed that they were extraordinary negotiators. They have become accustomed to getting their way.

Kleiner Perkins venture capitalist John Doerr was later quoted as saying, "I have never paid more money for so little a stake in a startup."[10] Sequoia head Mike Moritz said that the pair's "manic devotion" helped to convince him.[11] But he also admitted that he really made the investment because, if the search engine turned out to be good, he could sell the company to Yahoo, another company he had invested in. Sergey just thought they had negotiated a reasonable price in the Silicon Valley game of fund-raising. "I feel we negotiated a good deal at the time. They [the VCs] thought it was a lot, we thought it was too low. Angel investors treat [investing] as a hobby. The VCs do it as a business, or at the very least as a competitive sport," he said.[12]

Nevertheless, it turned out to be a spectacular deal for both VCs. After Google went public, each VC firm found itself with stock worth about $3 billion. It's possibly the biggest return on a VC investment in history. Once again, Larry and Sergey were right. But it would not be the last time they were to do battle with their venture backers.

With money burning a hole in their bank account, the boys from Stanford were on their way.

Chapter 3

Controlled Chaos

Innovators and men of genius have almost always been regarded as fools at the beginning (and very often at the end) of their careers.

—Fyodor Dostoyevsky

The place where optimism most flourishes is the lunatic asylum.

—Havelock Ellis

The Library of Alexandria became a playground for the great intellectuals, philosophers, and scientists of their day. Ptolemy ensured this by offering incentives. The library may have contained a garden, a zoo, and an observatory. Scholars who came to study there were given free board and lodging in the royal part of the city, exempted from taxes, and given commissions as tutors, often teaching in outdoor classrooms by the library. They participated in games, festivals, and literary competitions organized at the library. They were also, of course, given the liberty to study the scrolls and conduct research in their fields of interest. The mathematician Euclid studied at the library, where he may have done the work that led to the rules of geometry. Archimedes invented the screw-shaped water pump there; Eratosthenes calculated the diameter of the Earth, mapped it, and argued that it should be possible to reach India by sailing west from Spain. Galen wrote works on healing and anatomy that dominated medicine until the Renaissance. Never underestimate the value of perks.

L ike all great young companies, Google and its employees reflect the personalities and ideals of the company's founders. The way any founders keep their company's culture is to hire people who are like them. Larry and Sergey interviewed all prospective hires in the early days, and still insist on interviewing every important hire. The first person they brought in, Craig Silverstein, is a computer geek in their own spiritual image. He looks the part. Short and slender, with a Stan Laurel chin and a usually shy demeanor, in his spare time he runs an online fact site about Muppets.

But he's extremely sharp, and confident when he talks about Google and its enduring culture, which is full of young technologists who share Larry's and Sergey's ideals. "We hired people who were like us in that way," he says. "We definitely wanted people who were idealistic, and we've been careful to try to sustain that over the years."

Larry has put his desire to hire idealistic people this way: "We believe strongly that in the long term, we will be better served—as shareholders and in all other ways—by a company that does good things for the world even if we forgo some short term gains. This is an important aspect of our culture and is broadly shared within the company."[1]

These days, nearly every computer scientist wants to join Google. But in order to attract the best of them—in terms both of technical expertise and shared values—in the early years, Larry and Sergey had to offer more: a scientific and technological playground that any computer geek would love. That part was easy. They offered what every other Web start-up did when they still had money: employee perks.

Larry and Sergey have mostly retained the notorious frugality they learned at Stanford. They still buy the cheapest equipment they can find and modify it to fit their needs. Google does almost no advertising; new products immediately appear on the Internet in news articles and blogs. And when Google was young, they stuck with cubicles instead of offices, with desks made from doors—although work spaces were decorated with colorful streamers, paraphernalia from favorite movies, props and pictures of exotic foreign cities, fairy tales, anything that struck the fancies of the employees who worked there.

Employee perks are another matter. Google's culture has been described as "part university campus and part kindergarten playground."[2] More realistically, it's a young man's playground. There are the usual lava lamps, game rooms with pool tables, and foosball and video games typical of technology start-ups during the first dot-com heyday. But Google goes further than most: massage chairs, "sleeping pods" where employees can take a nap, and the famous free gourmet food and drinks. (Google lobbies usually have glass-front refrigerators filled with free Naked Juice for visitors.) Google is also famous for hiring a company masseuse. Recalls one early employee, "The full-time masseuse, Babette, was gorgeous. She gave 'naked under the sheets' massages."

Even in the early days, employees dined on free gourmet food: rack of lamb and rib eye steaks, Cajun food, scallops, as well as hamburgers and hot dogs, fish sandwiches, and salad bars. Free snacks were mostly on the healthy side: Odwalla drinks, granola bars, Yukon Gold chips, decaf coffee.

But the biggest draw for young scientists at Google wasn't the free food. Computer scientists and engineers were infected with the desire to do something incredible, the disease propagated by Larry and Sergey. Sergey has emphasized this fact, noting that it's especially important as the stock price retreats. "This is where you want to make sure you are hiring employees because they love to work here, they love to create things, and they're not here primarily for the money," he says. "Although when they do create something valuable you want to reward them. That's when these things really pay off." Employees agree that the opportunity to make a name for themselves even outweighed the perks and the promise of riches from an IPO. Not that everyone ignored the prospect of riches; it's a big draw for anyone joining a promising start-up. But it wasn't everything, according to one former employee:

> I had been at another dot-com, and left for Google. At the first dot-com, there was an excitement, but at Google it was a whole different kind of excitement. People were really sure they were on to something. At the earlier dot-com, they were thinking more about how they were going to be rich. At Google, it was almost disdainful to talk about money. It was hot and happening. They all saw the spending and instant riches, but honestly it was never a stated goal at Google. People were too focused on the technology. No one ever came running in with a picture of the sailboat they were going to buy. But they did come running in and interrupting meetings when we passed a milestone.

That employee describes the work environment as a "velvet prison," where the perks and friendly atmosphere are offset by the pressure to work insane hours. "Twelve hours a day, six days a week was typical," he says. "It was optional, but there was pressure to do it. They fed you all the time, so there was no reason to leave for food. Google was a twenty-four/seven lifestyle. And they were all such nice people."

The Stanford Brain Pool

Larry and Sergey used another technique to make sure they would get people who were as close to clones of themselves as possible. Their favorite place for recruiting in the early days of Google was their former stomping ground, Stanford University. Says Jennifer Widom, a computer science and electrical engineering professor at Stanford: "For the first three and a half years [after Google's founding], everybody who graduated under a faculty adviser in the database group either stayed in academia or went to work at Google. We used to joke that if Google went under, all our grads would be unemployed. Everybody says it's ridiculous how many Stanford alums are at Google."

For example, in 2002 Larry and Sergey hired Orkut Büyük-kökten to continue his Stanford work on search technology for hand-held devices. (In his spare time he pursued another pet project from Stanford and created Orkut, now the most popular social networking site in Brazil.)

Glen Jeh, another Stanford grad student in computer science, came up with a way to personalize searches to an individual's preferences, an idea he wrote up in a paper, "Scaling Personalized Web Search." In June 2003 he started a company called Kaltix to exploit that technology—some Stanford folks think the company was created just to be bought by Google. Which it was, three months later.

Most of the original work culture continues at Google today. Googlers enjoy subsidized day care centers, free meals, free laundry rooms, kiosks to drop off clothes for dry cleaning (employees have to pay for that service), and almost uncountable other perks. There are Google bikes parked throughout the GooglePlex that employees can hop on and ride from building to building. None of them is locked; employees simply take them when they need them. Some people bring Segway scooters, roller skates, or skateboards to work. A doctor regularly visits the Google campus so Googlers don't have to leave the office for a checkup.

And, of course, Google is known for its "20 percent time," the one day a week that employees can take simply to work on something that really interests them. They may start a new project, join one already under way, or put together their own teams. It's an irresistible draw, although some engineers say that these days it's actually hard to take the time to do it anymore.

Alan Eustace, senior vice president of engineering and the lead person on engineering hiring, explains the mandate, set primarily by Larry: "The important thing to understand is what the value proposition is of everything you do," he says. "Say we didn't have any cafés on campus. Then thousands of people leave at eleven thirty to beat the rush at restaurants. So you ask what's the value of those two hours, what interaction can you get if people are able to stay on campus instead? And if you're going to provide food on campus, what's the difference in price between bad food and good food? The delta is relatively small."

Larry and Sergey are also experimenting with new types of perks appropriate to a much larger company. A recent *Fortune* magazine interview with the pair noted: "They're tinkering with Google's 401(k) plan and making sure it's easier for employees to get financial advice. They're studying the effect of wealth on happiness, trying to understand what it takes to keep rich folks actively interested in their jobs—and making a contribution to the company. Page says he traces his interest in benevolence to employees to the rotten time his grandfather had of it working in an auto plant in Flint, Michigan, in the days of sit-down strikes back in the 1930s."[3]

Adds Sergey: "I don't think we should be looking back to our golden years in the garage. The goal is to improve as we grow, and we certainly have more resources to bring to bear on the cultural issues and whatnot as we gain scale."[4]

Strange Management

Larry and Sergey show no reluctance to experiment with unusual ideas. They have created a management system virtually void of any set hierarchy, with very few levels of management before reaching the top. People change jobs frequently, and for a time, project managers would shift jobs every few months in order to learn all the necessary ropes. Today they last about eighteen months at one job. Below the project manager level, people are constantly switching jobs. Engineers might be seen working at any time of the day or night, but mostly at night.

The company is also obsessive about having very small groups working on projects. Five or six people are generally sufficient to handle a major project—such as Google's book search initiative (more on this in chapter 9).

The interview process at Google is infamously brutal. Interviews are done not just with prospective managers, but with people in many different disciplines and management levels across the company. In engineering, Google has hundreds of hiring committees that meet one hour a week to discuss prospective hires. This system is designed to remove any biases from a particular manager conducting the interviews.

At the end of the process, after interviewees are winnowed down to the best, Larry steps in. "Larry still looks at every hire in engineering," says Eustace. He starts with written summaries of the candidate from the hiring committees, and "he'll poke at the ones he thinks he should look at. The fact that we review everyone means that nobody puts one over on us."

Larry's interviews are more likely to be an exchange of ideas rather than a question-and-answer session. In Eustace's case, when he interviewed with Larry in 2002, "he talked about in so many words organizing the world's information, how important it was, why it's an interesting technology challenge, and why search technology wasn't yet finished. We talked about the kinds of challenges that the company faced, about the company doing something that mattered."

The hiring process is necessarily constantly reevaluated as Google grows. "We don't really know that the way we hire at Google is optimal, and we're trying to improve it all the time," says Page. "We obviously hire a lot of smart people. We also hire people who have different kinds of skills, and we hire people who work on computers, and do construction, and many, many other things."[5]

Most important, the engineers they hire must have and be able to present a lot of information about a particular problem. Larry and Sergey like to run the company based on data. They pride themselves on taking a very disciplined, scientific approach to solving problems. "Their view is that information is the basis for almost all the decisions anybody makes," says Eustace. "The more information you can get, the more credible the information is, the more likely you are to make a good decision."

To that end, Google keeps a database of everything everyone is working on and sends out regular e-mails to keep others in the company updated. Employees—primarily engineers—are not only allowed to see what's in the works, they're also allowed to critique the updates (sometimes not very politely) and suggest changes. It's like a small town with a giant electronic network and too many computers. Everybody knows everybody else's business.

Eustace also explains the standard Larry and Sergey set. "The key element we're trying to find is smart people, productive people, people with a slight disdain for the impossible, people who have good leadership skills and who we find interesting. We try to avoid people that have incredibly large egos that are inconsistent with their abilities or are not good at working in teams."

The result of this craziness is that Sergey and Larry have managed to hire top people away from start-ups and established companies alike—including Microsoft. Says AltaVista founder

Louis Monier, "They've accumulated an amazing intellectual capital. For several years, when things were tough, they'd come down and get the absolute best people. They have the most amazing assortment of brains in Silicon Valley today. My old friends from [AltaVista's] research labs are there. They've just totally drained the swamp, in a good way. They have a pool of talent that is simply scary."

Many others in Silicon Valley see the brain drain in less favorable terms. Says one venture capitalist: "Google is sucking the oxygen out of the ecosystem for everyone else."

No Experience Necessary

Most of Google's new recruits come straight out of college or grad school. This is a trick that Bill Gates also used to build Microsoft. By hiring bright young grads, the company gets a strong intellectual base of employees who will work for low wages, accepting stock options instead, and have the willingness and stamina to work long hours. Generally having never had a job before, they are indoctrinated into the corporate culture. The company becomes their life. "The dirty secret of Silicon Valley," says one venture capitalist, "is that start-ups are run by single young people who can work all night. Google is recruiting only young people. The EEOC aside, it does seem to work."

Still, it's certain that the policy of hiring young people with strong academic cred has caused Google to pass up some very good talent. Geoff Yang, a VC with Redpoint Ventures, recalls a friend of his who interviewed at Google. He was in his mid-thirties and was highly experienced in online business as the head of Coca-Cola's interactive business. He went through fifteen interviews, and was finally asked to supply his SAT scores and college transcripts. He didn't get the job.

Larry and Sergey tend to discount the value of experience in hiring a new employee. After all, they didn't have any experience. Also, people with experience at other companies are not as likely to break the mold, to adapt to Google's unusual management style. Too much "context" for a problem, says Eustace, "can also stifle innovation. If you know too much about what's going on, you come up with twenty-seven reasons why this is hard."

That attitude can cause problems. In 2004, a fifty-four-year-old director of engineering named Brian Reid filed a lawsuit against Google, claiming he was fired from the company because of age discrimination. Reid, a former engineer from AltaVista, said he was told he was being fired because he wasn't "compatible" with the company's corporate culture. The lawsuit noted that Google's workforce had an average age under thirty and that fewer than 2 percent of employees were over forty. That case is still crawling its way through the courts. After being tossed out, a California state appeals court reinstated it in October 2007. The California Supreme Court agreed to hear the case in the future.

Until recently, few people left Google. Now that many have collected their stock options, some are bailing out, often to start their own companies. Being used to Google's culture, they can be difficult to work with. Says one venture capitalist who is now working with ten former Googlers starting their own company (all of them in their twenties): "They're young and brash. They think they can do anything, that they're infallible. They want investors to leave them alone. Which we don't do."

Two-Class Culture

Not everything is happiness and light at Google. As with any other company, there are the usual good managers and bad. When one online publication wrote about Google cutting back on perks, several anonymous people claiming to be Google employees or former employees wrote in with their own complaints—most of them with vitriol. One said that the famous 20 percent time is a joke, since their regular jobs consume so much time that they can't possibly pursue anything else. Another wrote about managers who never take on a task unless it will get them publicity.

Google's hiring practices and corporate culture have caused other problems over the years. For one, Google is something of a two-class culture. "Sergey and Larry are kind of contemptuous of non-tech people," says one former employee. "They're nice people, though they didn't always know how to be nice."

Some non-tech employees complain that they feel like second-class Googlers. They usually work in outlying buildings on the corporate campus, away from the central buzz that surrounds the founders and top management. The scientists and engineers, along with top management, get most of the stock options.

Still, some non-techies accept that it's just part of life at

Google. Sarah Bauer, for example, was an English and creative writing major at Stanford before joining Google's advertising group in August 2007.

She sees nothing wrong with the engineers' getting special treatment. "The engineers are around longer. They're five or ten years older. Google just demands such higher talent from them. It would be a little strange to treat me the same way, to have the same benefits."

Shrinking Benefits

As Google grows, some of its Pharaonic benefits are starting to shrink. For one thing, Larry and Sergey were too ambitious and naïve about how free they could be with the company's money. They thought that the lavish treatment could go on forever, no matter how large the company grew. In the prospectus for Google's initial public stock offering, after outlining some of the freebies the company offered, Larry and Sergey warned prospective investors: "Expect us to add benefits rather than pare them down over time."

They have not been able to keep their word. They even used to offer $5,000 to employees who bought hybrid vehicles—the vehicle of choice for both Larry and Sergey—but ended the practice after deciding that the hybrid market had enough momentum on its own.

In mid-2008, they shut down the free dinners at some of the cafeterias—those in buildings that don't hold the engineers. The reasoning is that engineers are the ones who work late into the night, while everyone else has a real life to go home to. Google spokespeople say that the cafeterias in nonengineering buildings were very lightly used for dinners, and it wasn't worth the expense to keep them open late. This event made quite a splash in tech blogs, whose writers were astounded that Google was cutting off free dinners. But the outrage was overdone. Nonengineers can still get a free meal when they work late; they just have to walk to an engineering building to get it.

In the biggest public backtrack, Google decided in 2008 to reduce subsidies for the extraordinary on-campus daycare centers for employees' children. When they first decided to offer on-site day care, Larry and Sergey opted to create the best daycare system venture capital money could buy. It's an expensive perk. The centers are based on a philosophy called Reggio Emilia, which advocates a self-directed learning program for those preschool Larrys- and Sergeys-in-training, an echo of the Google founders' own success at Montessori schools. They also boast highly paid teachers, small classes, and some of the best educational toys and learning tools.

This backtrack made the national press. According to a *New York Times* article, "someone at Google woke up one day and realized that the company was subsidizing each child to the tune of $37,000 a year—which nobody had noticed up until then—compared with the $12,000-a-year average subsidy of other big Silicon Valley companies like Cisco Systems and Oracle."[6]

Not only was Google spending three times as much as other

companies, but its subsidy was more expensive than getting a Ph.D. in computer science at Stanford, where tuition tops out at about $34,000. So they decided to raise prices to the parents by about $17,000 a year, making the price to employees a whopping $29,000 a year. Google was dropping its subsidy from $37,000 to about $20,000—still more than other companies, but for a daycare system that is much more expensive than others.

Parents cried, complained, and tried to get management to change its mind. This got Larry and Sergey to back off slightly on the tuition subsidy (they won't say by how much), but they did not change their opinion about the need to backtrack on employees' perks. According to the *New York Times*:

> At a T.G.I.F. in June, Google co-founder Sergey Brin said he had no sympathy for the parents, and that he was tired of "Googlers" who felt entitled to perks like "bottled water and M&Ms," according to several people in the meeting. (A Google spokesman denies that Mr. Brin made that comment.)

In short, as Google grows, Larry and Sergey have had to grow up and smell the perks, and the aroma turned out to be a bit too rich for a company with twenty thousand employees. Success is not entirely an upward spiral. The *New York Times* reporter concluded that Google was becoming "just another company."

Eustace defends Larry's and Sergey's decision to cut back on perks, saying, "Over time a small number of perks multiplied by a large number of employees all of a sudden becomes a huge number. Look at bottled water per employee. Multiply it by twenty thousand people, and all of a sudden you're aghast. We just spent a million dollars in one year on water." Regarding the daycare subsidies, he notes that "the benefit went to a relatively small number of people, but we were paying more per child than a full-time nanny would cost. . . . The numbers just didn't work out very well. It's healthy for us to look at each of those things. I absolutely think they have a right to look at our expenditures."

This became more critical when the recession that hit the world in 2008 hit Google as well. For the first time, the company started laying off employees. It started with several thousand contract workers, temporary employees who do not work directly for Google. But in January 2009, acknowledging that even Google had to start watching the bottom line, the company announced that it would slow its frenetic hiring pace and was eliminating jobs for one hundred of its recruiters. It also closed several far-flung offices, although it's offering those employees jobs elsewhere at Google.

The idea that Google is becoming "just another company" is a bit of an exaggeration. But, as is inevitable for any company that becomes as big and powerful as Google, the sharp edges are becoming worn as ideals bow to practicality, with the executives conceding to some difficult choices. The company is becoming both tougher and softer. The same is true for Larry and Sergey themselves.

Chapter 4

Larry and Sergey's Corporate Vision

> He ne'er is crown'd
> With immortality, who fears to follow
> Where airy voices lead.
>
> —John Keats

I n January 1999, a reporter knocked on the door of a Menlo Park apartment that had a handwritten sign reading "Google World Headquarters" hanging by the doorbell. Larry and Sergey had gotten their first investment from Andy Bechtolsheim just five months earlier, and the seven-person start-up was still working out of the apartment's kitchen and garage. ("Starting Monday, we'll have 6 full-time employees. This week we have 5, last week we had 4. I think it's going to keep growing at that pace for a while," said Sergey.)[1] The reporter, Karsten Lemm, wasn't looking to profile an incredibly promising start-up. Larry and Sergey were just two of several entrepreneurs he was interviewing as part of a story for the German news magazine *Stern* about Silicon Valley and the start-ups that kept springing up like poppies in the spring. Larry Page's business card then said he was CEO of "Google!"—that exclamation mark a sign that the pair aspired to be as important as "Yahoo!"

Larry and Sergey talked with Lemm about the start of the company, getting funding, and why they weren't late to the search engine game, with Sergey adding a telling comment: "There's one more important thing, and that's to bring what we've done to the world. That's very exciting, too, of course. And we think this does have a potential to really change things forever."

Entrepreneurship is a crime of passion. It requires motive, means, and opportunity. The opportunity that was handed to Google was appreciated by nobody but its founders until it was too late to imitate. The means and the motive are pure Larry and Sergey. Google is one of those companies that, like Apple and Microsoft, relies so heavily on the founders that, without them, it just wouldn't have the dynamism that makes it great.

Theoretically, any of a half dozen companies in business in 1999 could have been where Google is today. Yahoo was the leading Internet company and the main source of finding information on the Web (although it was not a search engine at the time). Microsoft had reached into its very deep pockets to take over the Web browser business and launch the Web site MSN, and was boasting that it was now Internet savvy. The search engine Ask Jeeves had a multibillion-dollar valuation.

But in reality, none of them could have been Google. They

didn't have Larry and Sergey or their deep understanding of the Internet, their evangelical zeal and dedication to "the search" as the savior of the Internet. Larry and Sergey had instincts that pointed them in the right direction, like an arrow flying toward dead center of a target. Those traits are what made Google so damnably successful.

They're also frustratingly stubborn, bold to the point of recklessness, and imbued with the sense of the infallibility of youth. They were the right people at the right time, online technologists at the start of the Internet Age.

But it wasn't just Larry's and Sergey's dedication to search that made the difference. They made the right business decisions as well. The surprising thing is that they succeeded despite their lack of previous business experience. Before starting Google, the sum total of that experience was the semester Larry spent working at a bagel stand at the University of Michigan.

And yet, in ten years they managed to turn Google into a corporation with twenty thousand employees and $20 billion in revenues. That ratio of revenues per employee, at $1 million each, is one of the highest in the technology world. (Microsoft weighs in at about $700,000 per employee.)

Larry and Sergey clearly did something right. That thing is based on their idealism and killer instincts. The mission statement they included in the prospectus for their public offering in 2004 was "To do great things for the world." They knew, unlike most other companies that provided search and portal services, that there was a huge need for a better way to search, that they had it, and that it was important. This attitude has dominated their thinking from the beginning.

Some people argue with the use of the term *idealistic*. In fact, Google's first proclaimed mission statement did not mention doing great things for the world. Before June 1999, the mission statement hastily put up on the company's Web site merely said, "To make it easier to find high-quality information on the Web."[2]

But even that mission statement works. Finding high-quality information *is* something that changes the world. The key thing is that Larry and Sergey were dedicated to the mission, without compromise.

When they filed for their first public stock offering in 2004, Sergey and Larry included the following statement in a letter to Wall Street: "Searching and organizing all the world's information is an unusually important task that should be carried out by a company that is trustworthy and interested in the public good."

Says Jim Barnett, the CEO of Turn, "They're really serious about building great products, the way Steve Jobs is. I wouldn't use the word *idealistic*, but they're on a mission and will stay true to their vision. They're authentic and committed and values-driven."

That attitude spread from Larry and Sergey through the rest of the company, and has not changed. Craig Silverstein, Google's first employee, describes it this way: "I believe we're enabling the Information Age to continue to grow and continue to be useful. There is great potential for good there. My guess is that most people [at Google] would say something similar to that."

Could the founders have possibly imagined Google would get as big as it has? Yes, says Silverstein. He recalls a conversation with Larry as Google was just getting started: "I remember once saying something like, 'Yeah, if we got this deal, and some other deals, maybe we can be a ten-million-dollar company.' Larry said we should be a ten-*billion*-dollar company. I thought he was joking. But now I don't think he was. [Larry and Sergey] have always thought big, and always had this idea that they would succeed in this business."

Modesty was never one of their strong points.

Just Another Stanford Thing

As a couple of kids from Stanford, hiring Stanford alums, Larry and Sergey were written off by competitors as unimportant. Louis Monier, the cofounder of AltaVista, recalls the attitude at the time: "This is just another Stanford thing." Monier felt the same way. "The feeling when I first met Larry and Sergey was that these kids are trying, but the market is saturated. I don't think anybody took the Google guys very seriously. Nobody noticed that Google's traffic was going up. Nobody paid any attention until they started to get some real money, and early adopters started moving to Google."

Ironically for a company that makes all its money from advertising, Larry and Sergey never followed the typical dot-com strategy of spending their VC money to advertise themselves into public awareness. They did put up a few small banner ads on sites such as WashingtonPost.com, in exchange for search support. They also went to a couple of trade shows.

But when they started the company, their disciplined frugality meant avoiding expensive ad campaigns. "We've resisted the temptation to have big advertising campaigns," Sergey said in 2000. "I'm not sure it's the right thing to do. I am concerned about long-term profitability."[3] So they turned to the Internet itself to spread word of their technology. The key was simply to get their product in the hands of early adopters, influential people who would recommend it to others and make it seem like the thing that cool people wanted to use. In those days, Larry and Sergey met in person with early adopters to tell their story. They had huge enthusiasm and great instincts about how to get Google known; they would tell journalists and other influential writers online to conduct vanity searches on the writers' names, impressing them with the fact that Google would find articles for them that they had written. Appealing to reporters' egos was a surefire hit.

They created so much buzz that they made *Google* a verb. Yahoo had spent millions of dollars on clever television commercials asking, "Do you Yahoo?" But nobody ever said they did.

As it turned out, this approach made it unnecessary for Google to advertise. The company grew so quickly by word of e-mail and online commentary that Larry and Sergey never had to spend the money.

An abundance of observers are ready to offer opinions on why

Google ended up as the most important, fastest-growing company on the Internet. Many, of course, believe it was Google's technical superiority that gave the company an enormous head start. "Their idea of PageRank—let the people who publish on the Web vote on popular sites—was an excellent idea," says Monier. "The Page-Rank idea is absolutely brilliant. It makes a huge difference."

But counting links is something that any search engine could have done. When he created PageRank, Larry, remember, was inspired by AltaVista's ability to track links. The difference is that Larry and Sergey recognized that importance while everyone else in technology overlooked it.

Competitors, however, generally claim that PageRank was no big deal. Says Robert Davis, the former CEO of the search engine Lycos, "A lot of people talk about their great technology, and frankly, I think that had little to do with their success. PageRank was not that innovative. Lycos did the same thing; it was the core of Lycos's technology."

Eric Brewer, a computer science professor at UC Berkeley who was one of the creators of the search engine Inktomi, echoes those thoughts. "Most of what is written about Google is inaccurate. For one, that PageRank was what made them successful. It's a lot of hogwash. It's very important to have an invention and market it, but it's just marketing."

This view has some merit. At the very least, PageRank wasn't the only thing that put Google ahead. There's always an element of luck involved in any successful start-up, and Larry and Sergey had their share. For one, they walked into a huge vacuum in the market, and were buoyed by their own hubris and single-minded obsession. They had complete faith that search alone would make a great company at a time when every other company that professed to do search was giving up on it.

The problem was that nobody had figured out how to commercialize a search engine. The prevailing view was that the flaw of a search engine was that it simply sent users away from their sites—and the ads they hoped visitors would click on. This started the age of "portals," a misnomer that implies a door to the Internet but was really something of a "walled garden" in which searchers would (the companies hoped) linger before heading off to other sites. All of the portals, including AOL and Yahoo, focused instead on providing as much content in their portals as possible. They had no incentive to build a better search engine and had largely given up on trying to improve the technology.

Larry and Sergey knew that this was the wrong approach. To them, finding the right information through a search engine is much more important than having a single portal trying to produce all the content that meets users' needs. The other search engines, said Sergey, "lost sight of that. It's why we started Google in the first place. . . . We want to get you out of Google and to the right place as fast as possible."[4]

Andrew Anker, cofounder of Wired Digital, which created the HotBot search engine (he's now at blogging company Six Apart), puts it another way: "The lucky thing for Google is that the others messed up."

Simplicity in a Complex World

True, but how did Larry and Sergey avoid messing up? By following their ideas of what a search engine should be, without compromise. Some of the things they did were quite simple, and quite by accident. These included creating a clean, spare home page with nothing on it but a search box and thirteen words. "The end result is it became a wonderful consumer experience," says Davis. "It was clean, it was quick, it was easy."

Web design expert Jakob Nielsen had been preaching for years that this was exactly how Web pages should be designed, because most people are lost in a maze of confusing technology, and they pine for simplicity. Even today, most professional Web sites are so cluttered with ads, pictures and video, and busy text that it's hard to find what you're looking for. Simplicity is one of the differences that make products from Google and Apple so popular.

The early team at Google quickly learned how important a simple design was. Marissa Mayer, VP of Search Products and User Experience, describes in a company blog entry an unusual response she started getting from one Google fan. Late one night in the summer of 2000, she came across an e-mail that consisted of just a number: 37. She had no idea what it meant. So she searched through her e-mails to see what other mail that person had sent. They were all single numbers: 33, 53, and then one that she found very telling: "61, getting a bit heavy, aren't we?" The first e-mail added a comment: "What happened to the days of 13?" She also realized that each message arrived on the day she launched changes in the home page. The e-mailer was counting words on the page and complaining that it was getting too cluttered.

Mayer thought she was doing everything she could to keep the home page simple, but she had never thought to count the words. That has been her approach ever since. The current number is 28. Larry and Sergey now insist that this is the maximum they will allow. In the summer of 2008, Mayer wanted to add the word *privacy* as a link to the company's privacy policy. But, she writes in her blog, "Larry and Sergey told me we could only add this to the homepage if we took a word away—keeping the 'weight' of the homepage unchanged at 28." She looked at the copyright line at the bottom of the page and decided to drop the word *Google*, since the owner of the copyright was obvious.

The important thing is that Mayer and other senior employees know what Larry and Sergey want, and know that the duo's final decision on any important issue is usually the right one. No other search engine even tried the spare approach to Web design until Google showed them the way. And once Sergey and Larry found that it worked, they carried it through to every search results page—something that virtually no other Web site has found the need to do. Just try typing www.yahoo.com and www.google.com into a browser and compare the results.

Focus on the User (Duh)

This simple idea is part of another quirk Larry and Sergey have: putting their users' needs ahead of everything else. It's rule number one that Larry and Sergey list under the heading "Our Philosophy" on the company Web site: "Focus on the user and everything else will follow." Larry and Sergey knew what people on the Internet hated—ads disguised as search results; intrusive pop-up ads; messy and noisy Web sites. Offering more of the same would simply not serve the interests of their users.

It's a cliché to promise that the customer always comes first. Any corporate executive you ask will claim this philosophy as his company's own. But the sad truth is that amazingly few follow it. Ask anyone who has waited for a cable company to get her system running, or wandered the aisles of a superstore looking for the item she wanted to buy, or sat on hold for an hour waiting for a customer support staff that has been cut back because business is slowing in a bad economy. Most retail stores follow a different philosophy. They study what items people tend to buy together, from bread and peanut butter to tissues and makeup, in order to figure out how to arrange these items most effectively on the shelves. But effectiveness is not measured by how efficiently customers can find the items. It's measured in how long it takes customers to wander the aisles in search of what they want, under the premise that the longer people wander the store, the more likely they are to find and buy something they didn't know they wanted. Larry and Sergey are dedicated to a simple idea: making things simple and straightforward.

Seemingly, the focus on users comes at the expense of advertisers. Larry and Sergey insist that the site sports a limited number of ads, and that each must be limited to a few lines of text with no multimedia enhancements. That is for the benefit of users. It's another way to keep the site simple and allow users to focus on what they came to do—find great search results.

But it turned out to be great for advertisers as well, contrary to conventional wisdom. Restricting the number of ads and making them easy to see makes each ad stand out more and gets people to click on them more often. Many critics insist that most Google users can't tell the difference between ads and search results. This drove up the bids on ad placements, creating an unexpectedly rich revenue stream for Google.

At the time Google was launched, the other search engines made the ads as intrusive as possible, displaying as many flashing, animated, and obtrusive features as they could cram in—a technique that most professional Web sites still employ today. The ads are a big part of the reason many Web sites today are slow to load. And people are more likely to shut off the ability to play multimedia ads or graphics altogether than to click on them.

Monier asserts that this philosophy made a big difference in Google's appeal. "That is absolutely the success," he says. "Search is about speed. It's a utility, it's a service, something that should be easy, available, very fast. All those things they've done. They've not compromised. By insisting on that approach, that's how they came up with the formula for advertising."

Controlling Chaos

At first, many of these decisions made no sense whatsoever to Google's venture backers. The venture capital community is a small and gossipy group. Several have told me over the years that Google's backers—in particular Mike Moritz—have fought with Larry and Sergey over these decisions. (John Doerr and Mike Moritz turned down requests for interviews for this book.) Just like any executives at a successful company, VCs get set in their ways and develop a formula for how to grow a company, and Larry and Sergey threw away the formula. Limit the number of advertisers? That was sure to be a move that would decrease revenues. But since Larry and Sergey had kept a controlling interest in the company to themselves, there was little the VCs could do about it.

The venture capitalists had one card to play to get Larry and Sergey under control. When they funded Google, the one concession they got was that the company would have to hire a seasoned executive as CEO. But the boys dithered on that promise for as long as possible. Frustrated, Moritz threatened to pull Sequoia's funding if Google did not conform. He later admitted to *GQ*, "It was not a pleasant conversation. In the heat of things, I rattled my saber loudly."[5]

In a 2000 interview, Sergey described the type of CEO they were seeking. "The model we look for is [Amazon.com founder and CEO] Jeff Bezos. He's very smart. He's a good motivator. Larry's better than I am [at that], and Jeff is better than he is. He's very fun, very pleasant to be around."[6]

Finally, in 2001, they found Eric Schmidt, a forty-six-year-old CEO at Novell and a man cut largely from the same cloth as Larry and Sergey.

Schmidt is a light-haired, mild-mannered, extremely smart man with a Ph.D. in electrical engineering and computer sciences from UC Berkeley. He wears John Lennon spectacles and looks like Lennon's nerdy opposite. Unlike Larry and Sergey, he also has poise, eloquence, and a relaxed, self-deprecating demeanor.

Schmidt first met Larry in 2000, at the PC Forum industry conference, when they appeared on a panel discussion together. Larry presented search results to show off Google, but Schmidt was unimpressed. "He was very shy," Schmidt recalls. "A nice enough person, but what I remember most was thinking that search engines are not very interesting and that he was shy. I clearly did not understand anything at the time of what was going to happen."

His first encounter with Sergey was over the phone. Sergey called him in October of 2000 because an employee they wanted to hire, Wayne Rosing, had listed Schmidt as a reference. The conversation started at 9:00 P.M. and went on for fifty minutes. "I had never had a reference check go on for fifty minutes," Schmidt says, laughing. "Sergey was enormously interested in Wayne, but

I remember noting that, just in general, he had this enormous curiosity."

That same month, Schmidt ran into Google investor and board member John Doerr, who informed him that Schmidt was on the short list to take over the CEO job at Google. Schmidt, who was CEO of Novell at the time, told Doerr he wasn't interested. Doerr kept insisting that he meet with Larry and Sergey.

Finally, Schmidt took Sergey up on an offer to visit them at their office. Schmidt agreed, he says, "just out of curiosity." He went to their headquarters, which was at the time, ironically, in an old Sun Microsystems building. The visit wasn't what he had expected. There was food on a little table and a projection of Schmidt's biography on the wall. "I thought, well, that's pretty interesting," Schmidt says. "It was not the normal way I had been dealt with in my career. It was one of those things in life you know is just different. Interesting and different."

The conversation was even more interesting. Schmidt didn't know that the meeting was a job interview, and it didn't seem like one. They debated many issues in technology, including a project under way at Novell to make a market for storage services for video, "which they thought was pretty stupid," says Schmidt. "They didn't say that but they basically argued against the premise." Their argument was there was a huge amount of fiber-optic cable lying unused since the dot-com crash, and if someone started using that cable on the Internet, video could be streamed live, thus eliminating the need for temporary storage. "I left feeling that something interesting was going to happen," Schmidt says.

At the end of 2001, Schmidt agreed to merge Novell with the information technology company Cambridge Technology Partners, and decided to step down as CEO, which left him free to join Google. He and Larry and Sergey negotiated through January. "Larry and Sergey seemed strange. They argued over all sorts of strange things. Every question was interesting, and every question was debated."

Although he did not understand Google's potential at the time, and insists he would have been happy if it had remained a small company, Schmidt decided to accept the offer. "I made the decision based on their precociousness," he says. "I had this tremendous sense that I wanted to stay because it was just so interesting. It was obvious that I should join Google."

Larry and Sergey insisted on spending a lot of time with any CEO candidate, which meant taking Schmidt skiing for a day. Schmidt thought this was ridiculous, and agreed to meet them at the Il Fornaio restaurant in Palo Alto instead. To test their knowledge, he compiled a list of questions that a CEO should know the answers to. The dinner lasted three hours. "They had good answers for everything," he says.

Just to bait them, he asked, " 'Why hire me? You seem to have everything under control.' Larry looked at me and said, 'We don't need you now, but we will need you in the future.' Which I thought was the right answer."

Ask Schmidt how two young men with no business experience developed such keen corporate instincts, and he says, "I think they were born with it. They had remarkably good judgment for such young people. It's intelligence, but also street smarts, insight. It's very impressive. It took me twenty years to develop the insights they had learned in two or three."

Schmidt has made a lot of progress in turning Google into a more professional organization, but without losing the ideals that make it unique. In his first year at the company, he wrote a list of standards and goals for himself that closely matched the ideals of Larry and Sergey: end-user happiness is defined by the quality of the search results. End-user happiness over advertising is defined by the quality of the ads. He also set the goal of developing Google's partnership programs to get others to use its search engine, and creating the corporate infrastructure to support a billion-dollar company.

Schmidt turned out to be exactly the right person for the job—mainly because his ego was sufficiently in check to allow Larry and Sergey to continue their radical ways. Few CEOs recruited to a small company would take a backseat to the founders, but Schmidt did. There are plenty of CEOs in Silicon Valley who will modestly assure you that they're not very smart, but most of them think they're lying. Schmidt doesn't play the part of a disarmingly underrated executive, he's the role model for the real thing. For the first couple years he acted more like a department head than a CEO. He saw no need to interfere.

Schmidt liked the fact that Larry and Sergey took an analytical approach to decisions, were proud of the company's technology, and knew that it was not possible to spend too much on building the technical infrastructure to support their ambitions.

"I didn't need to overshadow them," he says. "I'm a collaborator, and I didn't need the validation. It was their company and I didn't in any way want to take away from the perception that it was their company."

And besides, he did not think of his position as that of the ultimate boss. As major shareholders, Larry and Sergey control the voting rights of the board of directors, including the ability to fire the CEO. "Who works for whom?" Schmidt asks. "Do Larry and Sergey work for me or do I work for them? On the organization chart they work for me. But at the time I joined, they owned more than half of the company. Any CEO who walks into a company where the founders own half of the company and thinks those founders work for him is not paying attention to how a board of directors works."

The most important result is that Schmidt did not screw up what Larry and Sergey had started. Too many start-ups have been destroyed by CEOs, brought in as hired guns, who start conforming to conventional wisdom. "I think Eric is the only guy who could be CEO of that company," says Anker. "They are so over-optimized for technology. A standard CEO would be rejected. Eric can play both sides of the coin."

The venture capital rumor mill also says that Google's board was frustrated with Schmidt's refusal to rein in Sergey and Larry, but Schmidt denies that this was the case. In the end, it didn't matter. The three executives have learned to work together smoothly.

Today, Schmidt has become the public face of Google, while

Larry and Sergey have retreated into the background to run Products and Innovation, to decide where to expand into new markets and when to retreat. Larry is now president of Products, while Sergey is president of Technology, roles that keep them heavily involved in Google's future as the main arbiters of Google's technology. Larry and Sergey almost never give interviews or attend conferences. And Schmidt rarely attends the Friday technology review meetings headed by Larry and Sergey. Which is just fine with Schmidt.

Difficult Partners

Schmidt has still not managed to get Sergey and Larry entirely under control. They can be almost impossible to work with, especially when dealing with business partners. They're known for their reluctance to meet with other executives, showing up late for meetings and changing terms that others negotiate. "As negotiators, they are horrible to deal with," says an executive at another company. "Their approach is to push you to the point where you will walk away. They'd hold you over a barrel because they had the power to."

Not everyone at Google is difficult to deal with. Most of the people there responsible for relationships with others have a great reputation for being helpful and thorough. CEO Schmidt is highly personable and is involved—along with Larry and Sergey—in important negotiations, such as licensing the search engine to others and providing companies with ads. But Larry and Sergey can be stubborn. They know what they want, the ideals they wish to stick to, and the value of what they have at Google. "They're impossible to deal with because they're so convinced they are right," says a former Google executive.

It can be frustrating, to be sure. Some companies, such as Verizon Wireless, have a huge reluctance to deal with Google and are more apt to sign deals with Google's competitors. This could limit Google's future potential as it becomes increasingly dependent on partnerships in order to expand into new markets.

So, the more amenable Schmidt is taking on more and more responsibility for working with third parties. "Larry and Sergey are good at anything they choose to be good at," the CEO says. "Their role has evolved. Before we went public, they were doing everything. After going public, they retreated to work on the product side and the innovation side. Today, that ballet works."

It is, however, a dance that is still evolving.

Chapter 5

Advertising for the Masses

I have never made but one prayer to God, a very short one:
"O Lord, make my enemies ridiculous." And God granted it.

—Voltaire

In June of 2000, Larry and Sergey had a meeting with
America Online. AOL had recently merged with Time War-
ner, creating what most observers believed to be the most
important Internet property in the business. The AOL executives
wanted to get to know Google better and were considering licensing its search engine. Google had already garnered rave reviews
and, in terms of users, was growing faster than a baseball player
on steroids. But it had officially been on the market for only a few
months, and the AOL deal was huge for Google. It made sense
to link the two companies; KPCB was an early investor in both

Google and AOL. Although licensing their search engine was the primary means of getting revenue at the time, Larry and Sergey were reluctant participants in the talks.

"Sergey and Larry were mad that they had to go to the meeting," says an employee who worked at Google for most of 2000 but who, like most former employees, refuses to let his name be used. "They only wanted to talk to technology people. They were really socially awkward."

The AOL executives started talking about all the potential opportunities in the two companies' working together. Then one of the AOL business guys in the meeting talked about how Google was "stupidly" refusing money by not accepting paid placements—i.e., ads slipped surreptitiously into the search results. This was one thing that Larry and Sergey considered evil. Says the former employee, "Sergey walked out of the meeting and started screaming so that everyone in the meeting could hear him, 'Someone get me a can of gasoline—I have to light myself on fire to get rid of the scum of those people.'"

So much for getting AOL's business—at least that time. In 2002, Google returned to the negotiating table with AOL to discuss the possibility both of AOL using Google's search engine and of Google enhancing AOL's advertising system with its own. This time Schmidt took charge of negotiations, and this time he was the one reluctant to sign a deal. AOL wanted a guarantee that Google would provide it with at least $50 million in revenue over the length of the contract. At that time, Google was bringing in only a total of $80 million in revenue annually for itself, was just breaking even, and had net cash assets of zero: $9 million in cash and $9 million in debt. "I thought we would go bankrupt," Schmidt says.

This started the first huge argument between the founders and the CEO, one he describes as "a significant marital spat." Larry and Sergey were ready to take the deal, and ended up arguing with Schmidt every day. Eventually Schmidt decided to schedule an argument every afternoon at 4:00 P.M. The scheduled arguments included Larry and Sergey, sales executive Omid Kordestani, corporate counsel David Drummond, and Eric Schmidt. But Larry and Sergey would not give in.

Finally, Schmidt decided to take his case to the board, certain that the venture capitalists who had backed Google would share his reluctance. He was wrong. By that time they had learned to trust the seeming recklessness of the founders. "I called the board members, and they said, 'Oh, take the deal. We can always get a loan against your receivables.' So we signed the deal on Larry's and Sergey's terms."

As it turned out, within six months it was apparent that Google would have no problem meeting AOL's demands. The relationship continues to this day. With that deal, Schmidt learned how influential and how right Larry and Sergey could be—although that hasn't ended the occasional closed-door arguments over important issues.

Saying No to Advertisers

In early 2000, though, alienating AOL seemed like a stupid move. Google's primary approach to generating revenue at that time was to license their technology to others. AOL was the biggest deal Larry and Sergey could have made. But the two had very specific ideas about how advertising should be done, and these did not include giving advertisers preference in search results—a practice known as "paid inclusion."

Since Google's inception, Larry and Sergey have adamantly kept ads separate from search results, while others have not. They regard it as deceptive to users, something that falls into the category of evil. It might bring in revenue, as users are fooled into clicking on them, thinking they are pure search results, but Larry and Sergey were determined never to pollute their search engine in that way. In 2004, Yahoo announced that companies would have to pay a fee if they wanted to be certain their sites were included in its index of search results. In an article in the *New York Times*, Larry compared search results to newspaper articles, which are supposed to be free of influence from advertisers. "Any time you accept money to influence the results, even if it is just for inclusion, it is probably a bad thing," he said.[1]

Google didn't have to even try the practice of paid inclusion. Revenue growth was fine without it, and as a private company, Google did not have to succumb to investor demands that it pursue every penny of ad revenue possible. By contrast, in 2002, all other Internet companies were hurting like kicked dogs. Yahoo stock was down to about $5 a share. Ask—then called Ask Jeeves—had seen its stock drop to 83 cents. At that price, someone could have bought the company for $30 million, shut it down immediately, and still made a profit, since Ask had $100 million in the bank.

"It's easy to say we should have been doing what Google did," says Jim Lanzone, a former CEO of the search engine Ask. "But it was fundamentally prohibitive to do that at the time."

The irony is that paid inclusion didn't even do much to help the bottom line. "The dirty secret is that it's not just bad for users, it did not make you that much more money," says Lanzone. "The chance of someone clicking on the sixth or eighth listing on a page was so unpredictable and infrequent, it turned out to be a long walk for a short beer. It turns out there's a place for ads, and it's in the ad section, not the search results." Ask later dropped the practice of paid inclusion and put the ads only in the separate boxes where they belonged. Yahoo still offers paid inclusion.[2]

The important point is that Larry and Sergey never considered the practice.

The Big Shift

This dedication to clean advertising was a key part of Google's success. In life and in business, change comes in waves, pushed along by major shifts in the environment. To evolutionary scientists, the impetus for species change is known as punctuated equilibrium, a response to rapid changes in the environment. To science historian Thomas Kuhn, progress in science comes in leaps, the result of a paradigm shift caused by scientific revolutions dreamed up by the Einsteins of the world.[3] To Harvard Business School professor Clayton Christensen, technology advances through the power of disruptive innovations.[4] In each case—evolution, science, or business—different entities are selected as having the right phenotype to prosper.

Larry and Sergey provided Google with the DNA that allowed it to thrive and become destined to reside at the pinnacle of the Internet food chain. Just as organisms that have evolved for a particular environment lose their advantage once the environment changes, existing corporations tend to follow the same path into obsolescence. In fact, many of the ideas that Google developed were simultaneously being explored at other companies. Those ideas just never went anywhere, their significance poorly understood at the time. When it came to advertising, Larry and Sergey got it. Their advertising plan was developed—or at least considered—before Google was even launched. In a January 1999 interview conducted by Karsten Lemm, Sergey stated that they were in the process of "preparing" ideas about how to make money: "One thing is we can put up some advertising. Another way would be co-branding. Provide the back-end search engine to other sites."[5]

But those ideas did not take the form of an actual formal business plan. In fact, there was no business plan, which would normally lay out in detail the proposed revenue stream, with projections on how fast revenues would grow in five years. "We worked on a business plan for a little bit, but we were basically never even asked for it," Sergey told Lemm. He then added, "Recently we got an e-mail from one of our investors saying, 'Oh, do you guys have a business plan? I don't think I ever saw one.'"

Although they didn't yet have any idea how the ads would work, they already knew one thing: the ads had to be useful rather than an annoyance. Said Sergey: "The key there is to put up advertising that will be really useful to our users and not slow down our site. That way we won't push people away from our site, but we'll still take in some revenue."

It took them nearly three years to figure out how to fill the requirements Sergey had stipulated. Silverstein says that Larry and Sergey felt that no advertiser on the Internet had solved that problem. It's likely none of them was trying. Just as Larry and Sergey demonstrated that there was a huge market for a search engine that gave better results, they set out to show that there was a market for Internet advertising that gave better results, with the needs of the user—not the advertisers—given the highest priority. "We had this idea that if we could get a lot of users, we could make money," says Silverstein. "That said, we did not have advertising for a long time because we couldn't think of a way to do it that we thought was good for our users. Which I think gets to what Sergey was warning about. There are a lot of ways to do advertising. It took us quite a while to find a way that was actually beneficial to users and have an appropriate separation between editorial and advertising. We noodled it over, we talked about it."

Larry and Sergey have maintained this attitude that advertising should be done only when it helps the user in some way. In

2006, engineers met with Larry and Sergey with a simple proposal: to include ads with image-search results. They argued that this would add $80 million a year to revenues. Larry's response was to ask: "We're not making enough money already?" Sergey was equally skeptical. "I don't see how it enhances the experience of our users," he said. They rejected the proposal.[6]

Inventing AdWords

In 2002, most advertising at the time, including ads on Microsoft's site, MSN, came in the form of banner or display advertising, flashing billboards that appeared at the top of the page. Some search engine/portals were already "selling" search terms to advertisers, charging them for making the ads appear when people searched using certain words. But most contracts set a predetermined price negotiated by ad reps, rather than using an auction. As CEO Schmidt puts it, the philosophy was, "Give us half a million dollars and we'll show the ad whenever it's appropriate."

A company called GoTo.com (later renamed Overture) had come up with the idea of an online Yellow Pages system, where users would type in search words and be taken to advertisers who bid to have their ads appear when people searched with those words. (In 2002, after Google started showing the way, Microsoft and Yahoo both considered buying Overture. Yahoo won the bid.)

Larry and Sergey started placing ads next to search results almost immediately, in 2000, but also sold them for a set fee. But they were not satisfied with that; they had to be sure the ads were as relevant to their users' interests as were the search results.

Google executives today insist that their approach was unique, and continues to evolve. "The idea came out of GoTo," says Google chief economist Hal Varian. "But [GoTo] didn't really improve it. We took their model and refined it. When the guys at Google looked at it, they figured out how to advance it. This strong emphasis on quality came from Sergey and Larry."

In order to ensure that quality, Google essentially created a separate search engine dedicated to determining the relevance of ads, allowing them to select from millions of ads before displaying them. "Larry and Sergey came up with the targeted ad model," says CEO Schmidt. "That model coupled with search is a gold mine."

The focus in the early days was small advertisers—a market that would put Google in competition with eBay online and classified advertisers in newspapers. It fit well with Larry's and Sergey's desire to focus on small players and individuals. The two founders believe in the idea of the "long tail," all the millions of people on the Internet who wanted services that were not being offered by others. In Google's 2006 annual report to shareholders, Sergey discussed the importance of small advertisers: "Our goal is to create a single and complete advertising system. Diversity in our advertising and publisher base continues to be central to our business and is important to our long-term success. Advertisers large and small use Google to reach their target audiences easily and get measurable ROI [return on investment]. . . . As more and more users look for local information online, we must continue to improve our ability to attract local advertisers. This year we partnered with companies . . . to help us bring more business information online and convert more small businesses into happy Google customers. Small business is big business."

Because prices were to be low, sometimes just pennies per click, volume had to be extremely high. This required a fully automated system with very little human intervention.

What they came up with was a system that would let advertisers bid online to set prices, with those ads automatically matched to search terms without advertisers' ever talking to an ad rep. "Getting to that vision of what [advertising] could be was the big bottleneck," says Silverstein. "We could run a system ourselves that could support having a million advertisements from one advertising company [i.e., Google] and just show the right ad for the right kind of search."

After some testing, it seemed to work. So in January 2002, Larry and Sergey gave the go-ahead to convert Google's premium ad system—in which fixed-fee ads were placed in a box at the top of the search results—with the auction-based AdWords program. Larry and Sergey were solidly behind the switch, but Schmidt was worried that the auction system would not set ad prices as high as those the Google ad reps were getting. "I said, 'Promise me that revenue won't fall.' I was terrified."

As a precaution, Schmidt instituted a period of restricted spending, also known within Google as the "crap period." The rule was wickedly simple: people could spend money only one day a week. Every Friday morning at 10:00 A.M., anyone who wanted to buy something had to head to Schmidt's office to justify the expense. But this lasted about three weeks. By then Schmidt had discovered that the ads priced through bids were collecting twice as much revenue as the ones that had been sold by the ad reps. It turned out that the reps were pricing the ads too low for the market. One of the beauties of Google's ad system is that it automatically reaches exactly the price the market will bear.

It was the support Larry and Sergey gave that made the difference. Other companies did not have the push from top management to take that leap. In November 1998, Microsoft bought a company called LinkExchange, which was in the business of distributing ads to other Web sites. Along with that acquisition came a man named Scott Banister, a young college dropout who had come up with the idea for something he called Keywords, a business he had sold to LinkExchange. His concept was to create a software system that would auction off search terms to advertisers, placing the ads next to the search results.

In early 2000, Microsoft's online group ran an experimental system to match search queries with ads. But some managers were worried that the system would eat into display ad revenue, so those ads were shoved to the bottom of the page, and minimum bids were placed at fifteen dollars per ad. In May the service was shut down. Despite the fact that Banister's boss, Ali Partovi, pitched the concept to Microsoft as "the next big thing," executives at Microsoft rejected the idea.[7] They were too tied to banner ads. Microsoft executive Satya Nadella later admitted that shutting off the service was, in retrospect, "a terrible decision. But in all honesty, none of us saw the paid-search model in all its glory."[8]

Microsoft wasn't the only company to reject the idea of so-called "search advertising" as a revenue model. Partovi, frustrated with his lack of progress at Microsoft, started shopping the idea to others. Yahoo also turned him down. So he tried Google. But Larry and Sergey had already started pursuing the idea on their own.

The Scientific Approach

CEO Eric Schmidt has also made significant contributions to the development of Google's advertising system. The biggest may be in luring economist Hal Varian to the company.

Varian, a sandy-haired professorial type with Bill Gates glasses, was dean of the business school at UC Berkeley in 2002. He had written *Information Rules: A Strategic Guide to the Network Economy*, a book that discusses how to market and distribute goods in the network economy, including how to price them. He had also been involved with Inktomi, the search engine that spun out of the university. When he ran into his old friend Eric Schmidt at a Super Bowl party in January 2002, Schmidt, who had read Varian's book, said, " 'Why don't you take a look at this ad auction?' " Varian recalls. " 'I think it might make us a little money.' "

Varian wasn't sure he was impressed enough with Google

to make the leap from academia. That spring, Schmidt and Larry met up with him at a conference for big thinkers at the Aspen Institute. Varian wondered who the young man was with Schmidt. "I thought, gee, why did Eric bring this kid along? He could have been in high school, as far as I was concerned."

But the two persuaded him to meet with some people at Google the following April, and in May, Varian took an academic leave from Berkeley to consult for Google.

In 2007 he became the company's chief economist. "It's a lot more fun here than at Berkeley," he says.

One of Varian's areas of expertise was predictive pricing. He worked on a system that could predict the rate at which people would click on ads and compare it to the bids people placed. It's part of a discipline called economic mechanism design, and it includes elements of game theory. The system allows advertisers to decide how much to bid based on the number of predicted clicks on an ad. This is an important feature, since advertisers pay their bid price to Google only when somebody clicks on their ads. In order to make the system more efficient for advertisers, they are allowed to see where they stand in the rankings and the bids made by other advertisers.

Larry and Sergey did not scrimp on investing in the technology to handle the ad placement system. "I've got to say, they thought big," Varian says. "They built a very large and complex system. It was significantly more ambitious than the competition's."

And this was at a time when they spent little money on the normal accoutrements of a growing company. "Most of their money went into the servers," Varian recalls. "There were still five people to an office, with desks made from doors and steel legs. That was mostly Larry. He plays his cards close to his chest. When [Larry and Sergey] started to understand the potential of auctions, the way growth was going on, they didn't move into bigger offices. The goal was to fly beneath the radar as long as possible. People were very surprised when numbers were released about how profitable Google was."

Larry's famous secrecy, however, was something an academic researcher was not accustomed to. The system Varian first worked out in the summer of 2002 was used internally, but was not publicized, or even written up in academic papers. But he was invited to give a talk at Stanford, and was allowed to say a little about the work, since it was a small class. A visiting professor there, Mark Schwartz, had been working on a similar idea, and talked to Varian about it. "It became pretty clear that he was going down the same path," Varian says. So after his talk, he went back to Google and reported that other researchers were working on the same ideas, and asked if he could publish a research paper on the work. "It went all the way to the top, to Larry and Sergey," he says, and they finally gave their approval.

Still, other companies were slow to catch on. A couple of years later Varian presented the ideas to a Yahoo executive. "He said, 'What?'" Varian recalls. "He had never thought about it. That amazed me, because we knew about this in 2002." After that, Yahoo hired its own chief economist, as did Microsoft.

The advertising system designed at Google has another clever quirk. Instead of just giving the highest ad placement to the high-est bidder, Google created a feedback loop to give preference to the most effective ad, not the priciest. Each ad builds up a reputation. If people don't click on it, it drops in the rankings, while lower-cost ads rise. Google executives have said the reason for this is to ensure that the ads are as relevant to the users as possible. But, once again, it turns out to be the most profitable approach. It's better to get many clicks on a low-paying ad than none on a high-paying one. It's obvious in hindsight: keep the most-clicked ads at the top of the page, and Google collects more revenue.

Competitors, however, questioned the originality of Google's ad system from the beginning. In 2002, after Google introduced its AdWords program, Overture sued Google for violating its patents. At the time, Overture spokesman William Tell took a few well-targeted shots at Google. "We've spent millions on attorneys' fees and lawyers' fees," he told TechUser.Net. "We're not going to let some company with a bunch of hot shot program-mers come in and steal our best ideas." The suit was settled in August 2004, after Yahoo had bought Overture. Google was granted a perpetual license to the patents in return for payment in the form of 2.7 million shares of Google stock, about 1 percent of the company at the time.

Creating AdSense

In March 2003, Google launched a new advertising program that would place ads on other Web sites rather than relying entirely on ads that accompanied its own search results. This was the business that LinkExchange was in when Microsoft bought it in 1998, but it did not become part of Microsoft's business model.

Google's system used its computer algorithms to analyze the data on a Web site and choose which ads people visiting that site were most likely to click on. But it turned out that another company, Applied Semantics, in Santa Monica, had a very similar third-party advertising system, called AdSense: its specialty was also extracting information from a Web site in order to deliver more relevant ads. A month after it launched its own unnamed third-party advertising system, Google announced that it had acquired Applied Semantics. In a press release about the acquisition, Sergey said, "This acquisition will enable Google to create new technologies that make online advertising more useful to users, publishers and advertisers alike." From then on, Google's system was called AdSense.

The final element that made AdSense popular was Google's deciding to make it more profitable for the AdSense partners. Google started splitting revenues fifty-fifty with sites that carried its ads, instead of eighty-twenty, as was common at the time. The reason for this, says one former Google executive: "It just didn't seem right to Sergey." The split today is even more favorable, and competitors have had to follow Google's lead.

The result is that AdSense is also by far the most popular advertising system of its type. And, it turns out, Google can afford to sacrifice a high percentage of the revenues from AdSense. Its true value is in the fact that it creates a bigger inventory of sites showing Google's ads. This creates a virtuous cycle: with more places for ads to appear, more advertisers want to use Google's advertising systems, which makes more Web sites interested in using Google's ads. No other system can match the sheer number of eyeballs that will look at a particular ad, and there is little reason to go elsewhere.

Competitive Response

After Google set the pace, competitors tried to follow, but they were several laps behind. Microsoft started a project to create a new search engine and search advertising system in 2003, code-named Moonshot. Its search engine was launched in late 2004 and the advertising system in 2006. But by then it was too late. Advertisers were dedicated to Google.

It is now extraordinarily difficult for any competitor to catch up to the infrastructure and design of Google's advertising system. Google had too much of a head start and never stops refining and advancing its system. The system was obviously doing something right and filling an unmet need; Google has captured the overwhelming share of all advertising revenue on the Internet, and regulators and competitors are warning that it has become an Internet advertising monopoly.

Both Yahoo's and Microsoft's ad systems seem to be racing on broken legs by comparison. By the end of 2008, Google had captured about 75 percent of Internet search advertising dollars, while Yahoo held on to about 20 percent, and Microsoft just

4 percent. Google's revenue from advertising came in at $5.5 billion in the third quarter of 2008, Yahoo took in $1.8 billion, while Microsoft's online revenue was just $770 million.

In early 2008, Microsoft CEO Steve Ballmer finally decided the solution was to buy Yahoo, combining the two companies' search and advertising market share. Larry, Sergey, and Eric Schmidt didn't want to see Yahoo fall into the hands of Microsoft, a company that, despite its fumbling in the online world, all three executives are wary of as a potentially fearsome competitor. "The Internet has evolved from open standards, having a diversity of companies, and when you start to have companies that control the operating system, control the browsers, they really tie up the top Web sites, and can be used to manipulate stuff in various ways," Sergey has said in a clear reference to Microsoft. "I think that's unnerving."[9]

It took another meeting between the top three Google executives to decide on a proposal. Yahoo didn't have enough ad volume to fill all the slots it had available, so Google offered to fill those slots with ads from its own inventory, with almost all the revenue going to Yahoo. The Google executives saw this as a way to save Yahoo from Microsoft's iron grip. It seemed like a good idea at the time.

But they also knew that the deal could cause some consternation among government regulators. Microsoft was prominent among the competitors complaining that Google already had a de facto monopoly on Internet advertising. So the Google executives decided to approach the U.S. Department of Justice proactively in order to explain why the deal would not decrease competition and would be a benefit to Yahoo. There was no legal requirement to approach DOJ with the proposal. The Department of Justice normally takes on antitrust cases only when there is a complaint or when a merger might reduce the number of competitors in the market. The Google executives felt that their proposal was by far the better option, since a purchase of Yahoo or its search engine by Microsoft would clearly reduce the number of independent search engines by one. Google's deal would be limited in scope, nonexclusive, and temporary.

They were surprised by the response. Microsoft lobbied heavily against the deal as anticompetitive. Newspaper advertisers complained that it would raise the price of ads at Yahoo, since Google's ads tended to get higher bids than Yahoo's. Critics argued that if Google's advertising system displaced Yahoo's, there would be less competition, forcing more advertisers to just go with AdWords and AdSense, thus driving up bids even higher. The Department of Justice cast a skeptical eye on the deal.

The Google executives still don't understand the complaints. Craig Silverstein expresses this view: "That argument makes no sense to me at all," he says. "I don't want to say anything bad about those people, but I wonder how they justify it."

Silverstein points out that an auction system is the most direct way to match supply and demand. "Having more auction systems does not increase the supply [of ads or of places to put them]. It just increases the number of auction systems. It shouldn't affect the price of ads at all. This is very basic economics, the law of supply and demand."

But Google's arguments fell on ears that were primarily listening to other voices. And Microsoft spoke with a very loud and influential voice. It had already spent a decade learning how to lobby Washington while defending itself against federal lawsuits over abuse of its own monopoly. It knew how to play the game. Larry and Sergey did not.

An article in the *New York Times*[10] in 2008 noted that Microsoft had collected some strange bedfellows in its battle against the deal, including the National Association of Farmer Elected Committees and the National Latino Farmers and Ranchers Trade Association. Presumably, since farmers use the Internet, they were worried about a Google/Yahoo monopoly. The *Times* confirmed that the Latino Farmers and Ranchers took a stance after talking to the Raben Group, a lobbying firm that received $30,000 from Microsoft to lobby against the deal.

Google had put its own lobbyists in Washington in 2005, but inexperience and hubris made them ineffective. Larry and Sergey have a tendency to believe that, since they're clearly in the right, the merits of the deal would speak for themselves, and Google's efforts echoed Larry's and Sergey's attitudes toward dealing with outsiders. In the *New York Times* article, one technology lobbyist who has worked for both Microsoft and Google said of the latter, "They're renowned in this town for not returning phone calls and not showing up to political events."

The Department of Justice came down firmly against the deal and signaled to Google that it was going to file a lawsuit to stop it. Schmidt and chief legal officer David Drummond met with Larry and Sergey to give them the bad news. "I told [them] we were going to have to make a hard decision," says Schmidt. "I knew what the endgame was going to look like." They agreed to concede defeat, although all were unhappy about it. At 10:00 A.M. on November 5, just an hour before the Department of Justice was scheduled to file the suit, Drummond issued a press release announcing that Google would no longer pursue the deal with Yahoo.

After the Yahoo deal fell apart, Microsoft announced a new program that has been widely viewed as a desperation move. It is paying customers to use its search engine to find and buy items online. Web shoppers who sign up for an account and buy items found using Microsoft's Live Search "cashback" site will receive a percentage of the purchase price deposited into their account. When the total reaches five dollars, the shoppers can redeem their cash via eBay Inc.'s PayPal.

Who's the Monopolist Now?

Google has made it almost impossible for other companies to compete with its advertising volume. It cemented its position in April 2007, when it bought banner advertising firm DoubleClick for $3.1 billion.

At the pinnacle of advertising success, Google is in a precarious position. With the overwhelming share of online searches and online advertising, it has seemingly become a monopoly, and government regulators don't like monopolies. Right now, its advertising dominance is only online. At the company's 2008 annual meeting, Sergey used an argument that mirrored Bill Gates's claim during Microsoft's own antitrust problems that Microsoft was not a monopoly because the computer business is much bigger than just PCs. Asked about Google's apparent advertising monopoly, Sergey replied, "You are narrowly focused on search advertising. Advertising as a whole is much broader, and Internet advertising is much broader."

But Google wants more. Federal regulators are now keeping an eye on the company as it diversifies into other forms of advertising. And the company is as ambitious in making those plans as it is in anything else. Larry, Sergey, and Schmidt are now diversifying the company into print, radio, television, and cell phone advertising.

The obvious question is whether Google can leverage its online technology into something that makes sense in other media. But there's already a lot of experimentation going on under Sergey's purview as president of Technology.

The most promising new advertising medium for Google may be television, an area that gets particular enthusiasm from Sergey. In a conference call in 2007, he said, "The remarkable thing about television is, it's surprising, but in fact, [among] offline advertising, it's the one that's closest to Internet-level accountability and we feel we can bring much greater ROI-type accountability to television advertising, much as we've done online."

How would that work? Google has set up a relationship with EchoStar, which makes controller boxes for satellite and cable companies. EchoStar's boxes are tracking when and how frequently people change channels, and Google is analyzing that data. They're finding some interesting things about viewers' habits during commercials. Between 5 and 15 percent of viewers, for example, change channels as soon as a commercial break begins. Google can also keep records of individual commercials, tracking how many people switch channels after the ad starts and how quickly they do it. Google is using these data to figure out which ads are more relevant to viewers of which programs.

As Google learns how to apply its analytical technology to other forms of media, it stands a chance of revolutionizing many types of advertising the way it has done with online advertising. On one hand, this could revive a moribund ad business. On the other, it could make Google an even more powerful monopoly, and a more fearsome intruder into everybody's habits and business. But Larry and Sergey have no qualms about upsetting the status quo.

Chapter 6

A Heartbreaking IPO of Staggering Genius

Statistician: A man who believes figures don't lie, but admits that under analysis some of them won't stand up either.

—Evan Esar

oogle's initial public stock offering in August 2004 was supposed to be the event of the decade for Silicon Valley, the way a lavish party at Jay Gatsby's house was a not-to-be-missed walk on the wild side. The year before Google went public, word had leaked out that it had already reached a profit of $100 million, a blazing contrast to the IPOs of the dot-com boom, when profitless companies went public on little more than venture capital and a prayer. By the time Google filed for its IPO in the summer of 2004, its profit was over $300 million. Wall Street needed the brightness of Google's financial picture to help boost the market and raise its own sunken bottom lines, and they lined up at Google's door like drunken sailors moored on the shores of Tahiti after three years at sea.

In October 2003, Bloomberg summed up the sentiment about the rumored IPO, quoting Kevin Calabrese, an analyst at Argus Research in New York: "The demand is going to be someplace between very good and extraordinary," he said. "Google is one of the premiere names in the Internet."[1]

All that seemed to change almost overnight. By the time the IPO took place in August 2004, it had become the most derided IPO in memory. The price had been knocked down to $85 from an original range of $108–$135 when it was first announced, and the public and many large institutional investors avoided the stock as if it came with anthrax.

No wonder the public was skeptical. In the few months before the IPO, the press made the biggest turnaround in coverage of a company I've ever seen. The event was described with such phrases as "an extraordinarily high premium," "sky-high multiples," "based more on the hype factor than business fundamentals," and "harkens back to the late '90s boom" and the "excesses of the [dot-com] bubble."

And those were all from one article ("Before You Buy into That IPO, Search 'Lemmings,'" *New York Times*, August 1, 2004). Other headlines were similarly apocalyptic: "Think before you buy Google."[2] "Google This: Investor Beware."[3] "Google IPO? No, Thanks."[4] "Google IPO: Not Feeling Lucky."[5] (This last article states: "if you're tempted to buy shares of the company once it finally starts trading, which will probably be next week, here's my advice. Don't.")

The hyperbole reached fantastic proportions. The *San Francisco Chronicle* refused to give in even after the IPO, as the stock began its astounding three-year ascent, by comparing it to the overhyped, once high-flying stock of Krispy Kreme. Google didn't have any of Krispy Kreme's problems (many of them outlined in the article), such as federal investigations into its accounting practices, a sudden drop in earnings, and the low-carb diet fad eating away at the company's revenue. But, hey, Google had hype.

Despite the public pillory of the IPO, Google management still considers it a success. For one thing, all the publicity had the effect of getting even more people to start using Google, boosting its market share. "We made quite a few mistakes," Schmidt concedes. "But at the end of the day, the company went public in a way that generated so much publicity that if given the choice of doing it the conventional way or an odd way, I would still choose the odd way today. In the four months before the IPO we got the worst press we'd ever had. But the IPO itself was a marketing event. The *New York Times* wrote about it on the editorial page. Everybody had an opinion. You can't buy that kind of publicity. I watched our traffic numbers, and our traffic was exploding."

But how could the press have gotten the story so wrong? Blame it on Larry and Sergey. They were trying to do something right. Instead, they pissed off a lot of people.

The Wisdom of a Crowded IPO

Once again, Larry and Sergey decided to break the rules. There is a well-established method to the madness of taking a company public, one that stretches back nearly a hundred years on Wall Street. The unquestioned rule has been that it must be handled by experts. Before a stock starts trading publicly, private investors who supposedly know what they're doing set the price.

The investment banks all have a pool of professional investors, mostly investment firms that put up the money from pension funds, government organizations, and other institutions hoping for high returns on their cash. The investment banks that get the contract then take the executives on a dog-and-pony show to pitch the value of the stock to their investors, who price the IPO.

This isn't just a promise of what the investors think it's worth. They actually have to put up the money. The stock is sold to the institutional investors before the IPO. As soon as it starts trading, they may lose money if it turns out the public isn't so optimistic, and can instantly make money if the price is bid up on the open market. The competition to get in on an IPO—and to price it conservatively—is intense. But with enough investors committing their money, competitive bidding should set the price just right.

That, anyway, is the theory. In the late 1990s it started to go haywire. With rabid demand for dot-com stocks, the usual metrics for valuing a company no longer applied. Investment banks would take companies public and then see the stock double, triple, quadruple on the first day. This became a rite of passage for a dot-com company. If its stock didn't soar immediately, it wasn't considered a hot prospect.

But Larry and Sergey listened to unconventional wisdom. During the boom years of the late 1990s, one storied investment banker came up with what he thought was a better idea. William R. Hambrecht had cofounded a San Francisco investment bank called Hambrecht and Quist in 1968, three thousand miles from the financial center of Wall Street.

Bill Hambrecht left the company in 1998 to start a new firm, WR Hambrecht and Co., with the promise of setting IPO prices at the price the public was actually willing to pay. Instead of shopping the IPO to big institutional investors, WR Hambrecht signed up individual investors, allowing them to trade online for both public companies and new stock offerings the company handled. For IPOs, WR Hambrecht let its individual investors bid on what they thought the stock was worth. The bank then set the price based on the highest bid that would still bring in enough investors to buy all the offered stock.

It seemed like a good idea to Larry and Sergey. They liked the notion of taking control away from large institutions, which always got the best deals, and handing the opportunity to individuals. In 2002, they consulted with Jay Ritter, a University of Florida finance professor who has studied IPOs for years, and asked what he thought of the IPO auction system. He pointed out that it was less likely to present a conflict of interest. "I told them an auction would be best because the allocation of shares doesn't depend on what kind of commissions (a professional investor) generates for the investment bankers," Ritter said.[6]

Besides, Larry and Sergey liked the fact that prices would be set by the wisdom of crowds, the principle they use to determine search results. And an open IPO favored their primary constituency—individuals—over elite investors. "In general, Larry and Sergey don't value conventional wisdom the way I do," says Schmidt. "Whatever the conventional wisdom is, they're suspicious of it. They felt that if we're going to go public, it might as well be in a way that addresses the apparent unfairness of the process."

In a letter written by them for the prospectus filed for the IPO, Larry and Sergey explained, "Google is not a conventional company. We do not intend to become one. . . . It is important to us to have a fair process for our IPO that is inclusive of both small and large investors. . . . This has led us to pursue an auction-based IPO for our entire offering."

When the investment banks made their pilgrimages to Google in search of the Golden IPO, they found that they didn't like what they would have to put up with to get it. Larry and Sergey were treading on too many Italian leather shoes.

Grudge Match

In early 2004, Larry and Sergey sent a team of financial executives and lawyers, led by corporate counsel David Drummond, to WR Hambrecht for more information. Clay Corbus, co—chief executive officer at Hambrecht, says that the Google team was reluctant to make such an unusual jump. "There is no way this is going to happen," he says the team told him. "They went back to Larry and Sergey, who told them to try again and come back with the right answer."

One Google executive on that original team, however, says that this isn't true. They simply found the bank to be too small and poorly organized to handle such an important transaction. Either way, they decided to conduct a hybrid IPO, using the auction system, but inviting many banks to participate.

Their golden fleece status gave Sergey and Larry enormous leverage over Wall Street, and they demanded a lot. Not only did they want to bypass the investment banks' main customers to offer their stock to average small investors, but also they said they would pay only half the usual 7 percent fee demanded by the participating banks. Thus began a Caesar-and-Cleopatra love-hate relationship with Google. Reportedly, one large investment bank, Goldman Sachs, appealed to Google board member John Doerr, who was an investor in Goldman, trying to convince him to drop the open IPO.

Two of the largest investment banks, Morgan Stanley and Credit Suisse First Boston, took the lead position. Twenty-nine other banks, including WR Hambrecht, were also allowed to participate, as long as they allowed their individual clients to bid and participate, too. Interestingly, Goldman, one of the biggest and most important investment banks, was relegated to minor status in the IPO, leading many to speculate that this was revenge from Larry and Sergey for Goldman's trying to go over their heads.

Schmidt insists this is not true. "You typically don't have three top banks take the lead," he says. "Our IPO was such a unique design, we went with the ones who showed the most flexibility in getting the design to work."

But the overwhelming majority of the banks were reluctant participants, and they did something Larry and Sergey did not anticipate. Although they had to let in small investors, they had the right to determine whether an investor was sophisticated enough to participate. This was necessary, since if it turned out that the price dropped precipitously after the IPO, the banks could be sued for luring naïve investors into a risky transaction. Most small investors were rejected. Some reporters tried to participate in order to write about the experience but could not get in, even when using money put up by their publications. WR Hambrecht was the one that let small investors participate.

Most small investors didn't want in anyway. The IPO, which would have been enthusiastically sold by the banks to their institutional investors, was instead widely criticized in the investment banking community. I talked to one financial adviser at an investment bank participating in the IPO who said he was told to warn off individual investors because the whole thing was too much of a "mess."

Part of that reaction was simple fear. The banks had never done anything like this before and were genuinely scared of how it would all turn out. But part of it was just a reflection of their anger at Larry and Sergey and their demands. "Part of the reaction was Wall Street anger because we were doing it our way, not their way," says a former Google executive who followed the public reaction. "But part of it was fear in the brokerage community. Nobody knew how it would come out. It was a hassle for the brokers, and they encouraged people to stay away."

Larry and Sergey did make some mistakes. They never seemed to take the IPO process very seriously. Months before they set the process in motion, they gave a lengthy interview to *Playboy* magazine, one of the last they ever gave. By the time the article hit the streets, the IPO was already announced and the stock's valuation was being discussed. The Securities and Exchange Commission started an investigation into whether Larry and Sergey had violated the "quiet period" before an IPO, the time between starting the IPO process and the actual event, in which the company is not supposed to do anything that will hype the stock. The company is also not supposed to give any information to a limited audience that is not available to everyone. Most companies simply don't give any interviews before a planned IPO in order to avoid this problem. Finally, Larry and Sergey agreed to ensure that everyone interested in the stock would have the same information by including the *Playboy* interview in the prospectus sent to potential investors. It did not include any of the magazine's pictures.

They also didn't take very seriously their IPO tour to investment bank clients. They were more interested in talking about the great things they were doing for the world than in explaining the company's financial prospects. Their financial reports to the SEC included sections titled "Don't Be Evil" and "Making the World a Better Place." It made them look like amateurs.

To this day, Larry and Sergey refuse to follow the example of almost every other company and give "advance guidance" of future company performance to Wall Street analysts. They're actually following the intent of SEC rules that prohibit giving information to select individuals that is not given to everyone. Wall Street considers a company that refuses to give guidance to be a company in trouble. And analysts consistently do a terrible job of predicting Google's earnings before they're released.

The result of all this was to drive down the IPO price, which led Google to reduce the number of shares available for sale to 19.6 million, down from the 25.7 million originally planned. Larry and Sergey cut the number of personal shares they were selling in the IPO by half, while the venture capitalists who funded the company pulled out of the IPO entirely. One *Wall Street Journal* article quoted one hedge fund manager who decided not to participate: "[Google] managed to tee off the broader constituency of Wall Street, and it's obviously hurt them," he said. "Wall Street wins again."[7]

Nattering Nabobs of Negativity

The real problem, though, was that the press took the bait from Wall Street like hungry wolves looking for a juicy meal in the dog days of summer. The wisdom of crowds can only come up with the right answer if the crowds have the right information to start with. Says a former Google executive who followed the reaction to the IPO, "It's more important what the press thinks of you than what Wall Street does."

In the publicity surrounding the IPO, Google suddenly seemed full of flaws. First on the list was the specter of looming competition, primarily from Yahoo and Microsoft—despite the fact that both companies had been releasing new versions of search engines for years without this having the smallest effect on Google's increasing market share. Professional investors insisted that Yahoo was the better investment, since it had more sources of revenue than Google, which was entirely dependent on advertising. Yahoo was also supposedly more profitable than Google. Reporters expressed incredulity that the IPO would give Google a market value comparable to that of General Motors.

All these flags were red herrings that any business reporter should have known to discount. They should have known, for example, that comparisons to slow-growth companies in completely unrelated industries are irrelevant. When compared to Yahoo or Microsoft, Google's valuation was reasonable, if not overly conservative. Google's net revenue ($962 million in 2003) had nearly tripled from the previous year, while Yahoo's net revenue ($1.5 billion) had grown by 68 percent, clearly putting Google on a track to quickly bypass Yahoo.

But profit, not revenue, is the primary metric for valuing a company's stock. And there, the press got the numbers wrong. Every article said that Google's 2003 profit was $106 million, while Yahoo's was $238 million. That's what the companies reported. But the press—and apparently the Wall Street analysts—overlooked one important fact. The two companies applied vastly different write-offs to their earnings.

This was due to a decision by Larry, Sergey, and the financial team at Google to make their financial reporting squeaky clean before the IPO. Accounting rules require companies to write off different expenses before reporting net income, such as the depreciation of the value of the equipment they own. One of the biggest expenses is stock options, incentives to keep employees by allowing them to buy company stock at a discount. Yahoo had been writing off stock options for years. But, about to become a public company, Google wrote off a huge number of stock options in 2003—$229 million versus $22 million for Yahoo. Since many of these discounts do not reflect actual expenses, many analysts use operating income (before expenses) to value a company. In 2003, Yahoo's operating income was $296 million, while Google's was $342 million. Google was already more profitable than Yahoo, and growing faster. None of the Wall Street analysts or reporters mentioned this fact.

The press also soundly criticized Google for creating a two-class stock system. The common stock shareholders were to get one vote per share on important issues, while Larry, Sergey, and CEO Schmidt got ten. In their letter in the prospectus, Larry and Sergey explained why: "[T]he standard structure of public ownership may jeopardize the independence and focused objectivity that have been most important in Google's past success and that we consider most fundamental for its future. Therefore, we have implemented a corporate structure that is designed to protect Google's ability to innovate and retain its most distinctive characteristics."

This was seen as bad "corporate governance," allowing the executives to ignore stockholders' demands when running the company. The press neglected to mention that most of their own parent companies—including those of the *New York Times*, *Washington Post*, and *Wall Street Journal*—have similar two-class stock systems for exactly the same reason. Management does not want shareholders to pressure them into maximizing profits and stock prices quarter to quarter while sacrificing long-term goals.

And in their letter to shareholders, Larry and Sergey clearly warned prospective buyers of the consequences:

> We believe a dual class voting structure will enable Google, as a public company, to retain many of the positive aspects of being private. We understand some investors do not favor dual class structures. Some may believe that our dual class structure will give us the ability to take actions that benefit us, but not Google's shareholders as a whole. We have considered this point of view carefully, and we and the board have not made our decision lightly. We are convinced that everyone associated with Google—including new investors—will benefit from this structure. However, you should be aware that Google and its shareholders may not realize these intended benefits.

This did not go a long way toward making investors feel more comfortable with the stock. The business reporters writing about the IPO actually thought their reporting was fair. BusinessJournalism.org even reported on this conservatism as a good thing, quoting David Callaway, editor in chief of CBS MarketWatch .com, as saying, "The media is more balanced in their approach to the Google IPO than they were five years ago. They're reflecting a public that's been burned before by these tech IPOs."[8]

This time, the public was burned by a press that was overly skeptical, backed by a bitter Wall Street and Larry's and Sergey's refusal to provide any information beyond the prospectus, which took time and knowledge to analyze.

So what do Larry and Sergey think of the whole process? There's a clue to their attitude in Google's IPO prospectus. In that document, Google's original estimate of the value of the stock it would sell in the IPO was an unusually precise $2,717,281,828. Most companies round it off to the nearest million or so and the press reported it as simply "over $2.7 billion."

But mathematicians recognize the joke—the figure's similarity to e, a famous "irrational" number (one whose digits go on forever after the decimal point without ever repeating a pattern). Known as "Euler's constant" or the "natural logarithm," the value of e, rounded to nine decimal places, is 2.717281828.

In other words, Larry and Sergey tried to set their IPO price at a valuation of exactly $$e$ billion, to the nearest dollar. They have shown, in more ways than one, that any stock valuation is, inherently, irrational. As irrational, perhaps, as executives who put doing great things for the world above shareholders' interests.

Chapter 7

The China Syndrome

Google as Big Brother

It is unbecoming for young men to utter maxims.

—Aristotle

In February 2006, Larry Brilliant went to Google headquarters to talk to Larry and Sergey about a job, heading the company's philanthropic arm, Google.org. Dr. Brilliant spent a good part of the day in a room with Larry and Sergey, and talked very little about Google.org.

"We just talked about life and where they want to go," says Dr. Brilliant. "And they were amazing. I had never met anyone like them before. I hadn't worked for anybody in about forty years and was not interested in the idea of working for a big company. But with Larry and Sergey I changed my mind."

What impressed him about Larry and Sergey was their over-the-top idealism and extreme desire to do important things for the world. When he arrived at Google to talk with them for the first time, the pair had just decided to set up operations in China, which meant conforming to China's strict censorship rules. Thus Google had become a censor, and it grated on Larry and Sergey's conscience. It became the topic of their conversation.

"We talked about whether Google should be in China or not," Brilliant says. "Every question came back to, what's the morally right thing to do?"

The topic was a sensitive one for Google. "I don't think there's any big company in the U.S. that isn't constantly looking at its relationship with China," says Brilliant. "It's a huge business partner, and it's an unusual business partner. It has a series of pressures that we're not used to. We don't understand them very well. But whatever the issue was, with Larry and Sergey, it would come down to, what's the morally right thing to do?"

That's one thing that has never changed about Larry and Sergey. "To this day," says Brilliant, "we've been through a lot of crazy things, and never once has there been an issue where they failed to make the correct moral decision. They think about the moral issue first. Everything else is secondary—including whether Google will do well by it, or if it's good for business. I had never seen a big company in which the two people who controlled it had such an amazingly strong moral base. It feels strange to say that to somebody writing a book, because it sounds like puffery, but it's absolutely true. It's why I came to Google."

Yes, it sounds like spin, and the public is right to be wary of such claims. We're used to such spin control from big corporations such as oil companies spouting about the great things they do for the environment without ever spilling a drop of oil. But everyone who has had close contact with Google or its founders comes away asserting it's true. One former executive, with no reason to promote the company anymore, asserts, "Everyone in the company really does believe in it."

Define Evil

Increasingly, though, people accuse Google of "evil" deeds. The first question should be, what does Google mean by *evil*?

Sergey is the primary arbiter of what it means not to be evil. He has described it as a dedication to not taking advantage of customers as well as trying to do good things for the world. But it didn't start as a promise never to do anything that others might think is wrong, such as chopping down old-growth redwood trees to make a lot of money. It started as an internal mandate for how to run a company and do well by employees.

It first came up at Google when a few executives were trying to make a decision about a group of employees who did not seem to be working out. One of the executives turned to the others and said, "Let's just do this, but don't be evil about it." At another meeting a few days later, someone said the same thing. Eventually the rule was written down and institutionalized. Says Google economist Hal Varian, "It became something of a principle, not something laid down from above. It came about organically. It was about internal functioning. Later, when Larry and Sergey wrote the founders' letter to shareholders [for the IPO] they incorporated it into the letter."

Now Google is stuck with it. Everything the company does, big or small, is judged on whether the act is considered ethical. And, in fact, Larry and Sergey themselves have extended the definition to include business practices. On the corporate Web site, under the heading "Ten things Google has found to be true," the principle is number six on the list: "You can make money without doing evil." The part about making money is important. In the explanation of their truism, they did not write about treating employees well, but about the company's advertising policy: No intrusive ads; no pretending ads are search results; providing only useful and relevant ads. They promised objectivity and honesty, not fake search results from paid advertisers, a business practice employed by all other search engines when Google was started.

Some may interpret that view as one that says, "We're moral, and you're not." But Craig Silverstein, who has been with Google from its founding, says it's more subtle than that. "Larry and Sergey do not believe corporations are intrinsically evil," he says. "They believe, and Google's corporate philosophy is that, being a corporation, it's still possible to be an ethical company. You can be much more successful that way."

To simply say that Google has indeed been more successful that way understates the definition of success. Google's moral compass has done it well in an age of hyper-competition. But with the wide publicity of the principle that became described as simply "Don't be evil," Google found that it had almost impossible expectations to live up to. Says Andrew Anker, the former Wired Digital executive, "It was clear to me that they would push the wrong buttons. The issue is, don't pretend that you aren't evil." Anker believes that the sheer success of Google made it suspect. "Nobody can have a seventy-five percent market share and still be liked. You're going to piss people off, and those things will snowball. People want cuddly Sergey and Larry dolls. The problems Google is having is that the more warm and cuddly people are, the more disappointed you are when they let you down."

And they do let people down.

Liberal Censors

For one thing, Google—and all major online services—are voluntary censors. Larry and Sergey came to the reluctant view, against their instincts, that censorship sometimes serves their users' self-interests. To some extent, they convinced themselves of that concept. But they did so slowly and thoughtfully, weighing many facts before coming to this conclusion. "Larry and Sergey—all of us, in fact—have a culturally liberal view," says Google CEO Eric Schmidt.

"We all have to be in a room together. Larry says if it's something that's going to end up in the newspaper, we have to understand it." The sessions are not simply meetings of like minds. "Between the three of us, on any particular issue, we'll disagree on the details," says Schmidt. "We go around and around on the issue."

When the discussion goes around, it ends up in Larry's and Sergey's laps. A few years ago, when asked by a reporter from *Wired* magazine what defines evil, Schmidt jokingly said, "Whatever Sergey says it is." More recently, he told me, "The rule is 'it depends.' We don't actually have a one-paragraph rule. Our process is to rely on people with good judgment."

As computer scientists, they take great pride in relying on the smart people they have hired, as long as they dig up the facts to justify their position. Schmidt says Google's dedication to the facts is stronger than that at almost any other company. "An awful lot of businesses are run based on intuition, experience, all those things which we don't value very much. We value the analytical, 'prove it' approach. I'll make a broad criticism: a lot of executives look nice, they're smart, they're well-spoken, they give nice speeches, they use all the right marketing words, but they're not fundamentally insightful because they didn't start from an analytical premise."

Larry and Sergey get their experts to collect all the facts about these issues, then debate them in meetings and set the general policies. The executives responsible for the details then make the decisions on the particular issues, but with the approval of the founders, especially when they are controversial ones. While they don't like censorship and try to avoid it wherever possible, they have come to accept the difficult fact that it's impossible to do business in the world without it.

A couple of years ago, management refused to block the search engine from pointing people to an anti-Semitic site called JewWatch. Bloggers angrily decried that decision as essentially condoning evil. Sergey publicly defended the company's position as an anti-censorship stance. And, of course, all the publicity increased traffic to the site.

But sometimes Sergey feels the company has no choice but to remove material. Several years ago, for example, the Church of Scientology made a copyright claim against an anti-Scientology site that had excerpted text from the Church's writings. Sergey saw it as a free speech issue but had to back down because the anti-Scientology site did, removing the material rather than fighting.

When Google does remove search results, company policy requires that a notice be put on the site stating that information was removed. Google also publicizes what items were taken down by sending the information to an outside organization called Chilling Effects. Google forwards the complaints it gets, and Chilling Effects lists them on its Web site. Google often includes a notice on its search results page that there was a complaint and provides a link to ChillingEffects.org. Google is the only search engine that does this.

"The Decider"

Nicole Wong, Google's deputy general counsel, is the point person digging up the facts on censorship and privacy issues. Wong is a short, smart bundle of energy; self-confident, enthusiastic, and enormously good at what she does. Wong, whom her colleagues have nicknamed "the Decider," has considerable freedom to research and propose solutions to difficult issues such as censorship, having earned the trust of the founders. But she makes it clear that the standards she uses are set by Larry and Sergey—particularly Sergey—who attend most of the meetings where these issues are discussed. It's Wong's job to convince Larry and Sergey that her answers are the right ones. "The approach that our founders and Eric have believed in—and which I think is the right approach—is that when it comes to restrictions on speech, we should do so narrowly, in consideration of a wide range of factors."

She notes that in the early years of the Internet, when Larry and Sergey developed their attitudes based on pure idealism, the main constituency was the United States, Canada, Western Europe, and Australia, all countries with largely similar principles of freedom of speech. Google is now operating search engines in seventy languages. Censorship is not just a Chinese syndrome. China's censorship is just the most visible.

Wong clarifies the point. "We're now hitting a new generation of countries with both cultures and governments that are not on the same page in terms of freedom of speech," she says. "We've seen large-scale [censorship] efforts in Turkey, in Brazil, in Korea, in India. That's been a challenge for all of us [including all the other search engines]. How do we operate in the world and do it responsibly? China is one of the longest-debated focal points, but I really believe we must keep our eye on the ball in every other country that has similar instincts—which is to shut it off, to block the site, to take down that URL."

The German government, for example, demands that Google and any other Internet site operating in that country censor sites that publish or distribute Nazi material. Google blocks such sites from its German .de domain, but not at Google.com or other country domains. And the United States cuts short its free speech allowance when it comes to writings that promote violence, child pornography, and other illegal activity. Nobody complains about the fact that Google keeps its search engines from leading people in Germany or the United States to banned sites. The slope toward the abyss of censorship is almost impossible to avoid.

Censorship is a judgment call, involving not only government laws but cultural attitudes as well. Wong points out one dilemma that came up in 2007. Someone posted a video on YouTube that was highly critical of the king of Thailand, Bhumibol Adulyadej. The videos, which did not come from Thailand itself, were "unquestionably disrespectful," says Wong, showing the king with a monkey face, for example, or posed in compromising positions. But were they illegal? In the United States, where political and other public figures are regularly parodied mercilessly, they would be allowed under the laws of free speech. Thailand is a different story.

Wong traveled to Thailand to research the issue personally. She discovered, first of all, that Thailand does have a law against insulting the king. The king, who is eighty-four years old and was crowned in 1950, is deeply loved as an important, stable, and respected figure in a country that has been characterized by many coups in the last two decades. "The reverence for the king across Thailand is absolutely uniform," she says. "That law is a prime example of crystallizing the view of the people." When she arrived in Thailand, for example, an American living there told her that, to the Thai people, the king "is a cross between George Washington, Jesus Christ, and Elvis Presley."

Wong had arrived on a Monday, which happens to be the day of the week the king was born. Every Monday, the Thai people honor his royal color, yellow. When Wong walked out into the street, virtually everyone was wearing a yellow shirt with the king's image on it. "What that told me is, totally aside from what the law may be, the criticism of the king—which in the United States would be cast as political speech—had deep cultural significance in Thailand."

In the end she decided it was right to block the offending videos in Thailand. "I don't dismiss the validity of having different norms about what's okay for me to say to you in Thailand, or what's okay for me to say to you elsewhere. It's just different. And it's upon us to figure out how we offer a global platform that gets that right."

Wong firmly believes it was the right thing to do. "In offering our services, it's not just that all the information ought to be out there. It's also, are we respecting what people want to hear, what they're accepting of hearing? Or are we posting what essentially amounts to obscenity for them? I had to get to the country to figure it out, but I totally understand it at this point."

But the point where she draws the line is when officials try to expand censorship across national boundaries. Turkish officials crossed it recently when they asked Google for a worldwide ban on YouTube videos that violate Turkish laws by insulting the founder of modern Turkey, Mustafa Kemal Atatürk. At first Google responded to Turkish complaints by blocking the offensive videos only in Turkey. But in June 2008, Turkish officials demanded that Google block the videos worldwide, to protect the rights and sensitivities of Turks living abroad. Google refused, and Turkish censors blocked all of YouTube from being seen in their country.

A Difficult Decision

To the top management at Google, these issues illustrate the complexities and subtleties of the issue of censorship. And they're still learning. "I consider us to still be in our infancy," says Wong, "like we're going to take a corner too fast and hit our head on the wall. But this is an exciting time for us all to figure out how to get it right."

The decision to go to China was the most difficult one they made, despite the conclusions of Wong, which they ultimately accepted. Censorship should be anathema to a company like Google, and China is perhaps the worst offender, targeting dissidents, reporters, and political foes as well as banning sensitive topics such as Tiananmen Square, Falun Gong, and Tibet. In one famous case, Chinese officials demanded that Yahoo turn over information about one of its customers, a reporter who had written articles critical of the government. Legally, Yahoo had no choice and turned over the information. He was then convicted and received a ten-year prison sentence.

The debate over what to do about China started in earnest in 2004 and continues to this day. "For well over a year the executives—Larry and Sergey and Eric—debated what's the right thing to do. It was a very passionate discussion every time it came up," says Wong, who participated in the debates with Larry and Sergey. To them, it was a decision with implications that would "affect the future of the Internet itself."

In 2006, they finally launched a Chinese-based search engine, Google.cn, based and operated in China. The criticism throughout the Internet and the mainstream press was fast and furious.

Some of the criticism was off base. Many insisted that Google should just stick with its offshore Chinese search engine and try to get things past the censors as much as possible, rather than giving in to China's demands. Google still runs its offshore site, but since Google doesn't censor the results of that site, the Chinese government often blocks access to it using a filter known facetiously as the Great Firewall of China.

The founders finally decided that wasn't good enough. "A huge part of the discussion we had [internally] was whether we would have a chance to make a meaningful contribution [in China] by standing outside," says Wong. "With the blockage of the [Google .com] service in China, it was not just that you're outside yelling, it's that you're outside yelling and nobody can hear you."

Did Larry and Sergey succumb to the sheer desire to succeed in the fastest-growing and largest market in the world? It had to be part of the pressure they faced. China claims the world's largest population of Internet users—more than 253 million at the end of June 2008. Yahoo and Microsoft had already set up operations in China, and a Chinese search engine called Baidu was gaining traffic.

The market share of Google's offshore site started to falter in China as Baidu, which obeys the censorship laws, grew. In an August 2005 report, the China Internet Network Information Center (CNNIC) reported that Google's market share in China had dropped from its leading position to second place behind Baidu. Google's market share came in at 38 percent while Baidu's hit 44 percent.

At first, Google's response was to buy about a 3 percent stake in Baidu. But in January 2006 it announced it was opening its own operations in China, which meant agreeing to self-censor forbidden topics. (Google sold its Baidu shares several months after that announcement.) It turned out to be the decision that has done the most harm to Google's reputation. Across the Internet, bloggers denounced Google as having officially joined the ranks of "evil" corporations.

Once Google started operating on Chinese soil, it had to conform to Chinese laws, including censoring its own site, or face the consequences. Just after Google launched its Chinese operations, CEO Schmidt told me, "We have to obey Chinese law, or our employees there will be arrested and tortured. I have a problem with that."

A big part of the rationale behind taking the cold plunge into China was the idea that operating on Chinese soil would benefit Chinese users. In order to set up an office in China, Google's executives had to agree to block certain sites and topics from its search results, based on a list provided by the Chinese government. But this also meant that the Chinese Firewall would no longer block access to Google's site, giving Google more control over its site and ensuring that it would run more efficiently.

Google's executives also had the hope, perhaps naively, that more competition would help open up the restrictive practices of that fast-developing country as it moved into taking a capitalist and more international stance. Just the presence of the Internet, even under restrictions, floods every country with more information than it has ever seen before.

Says Wong: "Anyone who believes in freedom of speech has to think this is the most exciting time we've ever been in. This is the biggest democratization of speech we've ever seen, which means that you or I or my five-year-old has essentially the same platform as ABC News, or the *New York Times* or *BusinessWeek*. And that's huge, and it's fraught with lots of problems. It's somewhat on the paradigm of that classic diplomatic question: isolate or engage? At the end of the day we decided to engage, because we believed that being there would have more possibilities of moving things in the right direction than refusing to be there."

And perhaps Google's presence will make a difference. Unlike Google, Baidu does insert paid ads into the search results, which reportedly account for about 80 percent of the company's revenue. Press reports have recently alleged that those paid inserts include ads from illegal medical companies. And when the scandal over tainted milk erupted in 2008, Baidu became mired in another controversy, accused of accepting payments from the milk industry in return for censoring news about the scandal.

It is interesting, though, that moving into China has not helped Google's market share, which has continued to lose ground to Baidu. By late 2007, Baidu had grabbed a 62 percent share of Chinese searches, compared to Google's 24 percent.

But Was It a Good Decision?

The decision to move to China continues to nag at Sergey's conscience. At Google's 2006 annual meeting, shareholders representing human rights organizations began an annual protest, demanding that management reverse or reconsider their approach to China. Every year, the proposal is rejected. Larry and Sergey still own a third of the company's stock, with half the voting rights on board-level decisions.

At first, Sergey was defensive over China. At the 2006 shareholder meeting, the person raising the China issue argued that many people, he included, would switch to using other search engines in protest. Knowing that every other search engine already practiced what Google had just succumbed to, Sergey responded testily. "What search company would you switch to?" he shot back. The rights activist stammered over the unexpected question, then murmured that he personally used Yahoo. That was a mistake. Sergey was ready with his answer. "Oh, you mean the company that just turned over information about one of its users to the Chinese government and got him arrested?"

At the World Economic Forum in Davos, Switzerland, in January 2007, Larry and Sergey acknowledged that the negative publicity over the move had harmed the company's reputation. "On a business level, that decision to censor . . . was a net negative," Sergey admitted. Larry has displayed a more pragmatic response, believing that they made the right decision, even if outsiders criticize it. "I don't think we as a company should be making decisions based on too much perception," he said at the same meeting.

And at the most recent annual meeting in 2008, Sergey abstained from voting against the latest proposals to do something about Chinese censorship, proposals that would set up new committees to examine Google's censorship policies in China. He felt there was some merit to the ideas. But neither did he vote in favor of the proposals.

Sergey also clings to the belief that Google can make a difference in China by pushing the envelope of how to censor. When Google started its Google.cn site, for example, it took the extra step of letting searchers know that information they were looking for had been removed in accordance with government laws. "Even if we can't deliver that information, at least a user knows it's gone, that there was information that was blocked," says Wong. "That's a form of transparency Chinese users had never seen before. We're never going to be happy about removing information, but if we can make people aware of it, it's still moving the ball forward."

Since Google started that practice and got away with it, the other Chinese search engines have started posting similar notices, and it has become standard practice.

Wong also argues that foreign companies doing business in China, including Google, can't help but make Western attitudes rub off on the country's people. "We are employing some of the smartest computer scientists in China. They are working on hard problems and [are being exposed to] some of our culture and our mission as they do so. That's something that we will bring to China that I feel really good about."

And with effort, sometimes questionable items do get past the government censors. The lists provided by the Chinese censors are not always consistent, and leave room for interpretation. A study from the University of Toronto in 2008 found that not all search engines censor equally. When researchers tested a series of controversial subjects on the major search engines in China, they found that Baidu had filtered out 26.4 percent of the sites, Yahoo censored 20.8 percent, while MSN and Google were virtually tied, at 15.7 and 15.2 percent, respectively. An earlier study by Reporters Without Borders found similar results. While Google fared the best, the researchers at the University of Toronto's Citizen's Lab found that all of the search engines could be doing better. The lab found that 313 sites were censored by at least one of the search engines, but only 76 were censored by all four. Perhaps this leaves room for creating an independent committee at Google to examine more carefully what it censors.

Still, Google's management insists they offer tougher competition to which competitors will have to respond. Again, this does not apply just to China. "We have the same process for all of our other domains, even in the U.S.," says Wong. "Most of the removals in the U.S. are related to copyright issues. In those cases, we also put up a notice" that the item has been removed.

Like it or not, Google, with its powerful presence on the Internet, is becoming the world's censor. As a private company, it has the right to censor from its sites whatever it deems objectionable. (Sergey refuses to accept ads for cigarettes or alcoholic beverages.) It's unquestionably a heady responsibility for any company or pair of individuals, and nobody can be faulted for worrying over how far Google will take it.

Chapter 8

What About Privacy?

It's not a matter of whether or not someone's watching over you. It's just a question of their intentions.

—Randy K. Milholland, webcomic pioneer

The other important decision Google's top three executives argue about behind closed doors is how to keep their users' personal information confidential. People want, and deserve, access to information about government officials and other public figures, but everyone wants their own information kept from prying eyes. On this issue, Larry and Sergey come down like a falling rock on the side of confidentiality. They face vigorous criticism from outside advocates.

Google collects an enormous amount of information about the people who use its services, perhaps more than any other company in history. Google's computers track what ads users click on, what items they search, what sites they go to, even the topics they write about in e-mails. The information is used to enable Google's computers to figure out how to deliver more relevant data—and ads—to every individual. It's not all about Page-Rank anymore.

This doesn't mean someone at Google is reading people's e-mails. Hundreds of millions of people use Google's services, and humans can't possibly be up to that task. It's all done by Google's computers without human intervention. But the data is there on Google's computers, vulnerable to government subpoenas and, perhaps, to clever hackers intent on thievery.

To Larry and Sergey, collecting such data is all part of the process of making Google's services useful. But people are suspicious of their intent. Google could, for example, sell information to advertisers and other companies, just as magazines sell information about their readers to others. There is no evidence Google has ever done this, and Larry and Sergey promise the company never will—at least not as long as they're in charge.

Explains Larry: "Whenever you do a search, you're trusting us to give you the right things. We take that very seriously. We have a pretty good reputation in that regard. I think people see us as willing to take positions that some might find weird initially. But we definitely can explain why we did it, and we're up front about that."[1]

But if any government hits Google with a legal subpoena, the company has to turn over the data requested. Technically, such data do not identify an individual, but merely the Internet address of a user's computer. But the data can be used to find individuals—or at least those whose computers were used—by digging up the owners of the computer at that address through other means.

Privacy advocates and certain governments press Google to delete this information after a short period of time. Governments do so naively, believing that the potential threat is from Google's abusing the information; but it actually means it will make it harder for the government to snoop out illegal activity. The dispute Larry and Sergey have with deleting data is how long that period should be.

Wong says it comes down to one other reason Google collects user data: it helps determine traffic patterns that may identify cybercrooks, enabling the company to prevent similar attacks in the future. In this case, Wong again argues that preserving the data is the best way to serve users. "Focusing on users is not just delivering the best and most robust service, but also delivering a service that the user will trust. A component of that trust is about privacy because this is such a data-driven service."

Can You Trust Google?

User trust is an absolute necessity for Google, and violating it—or even the perception of violating it—threatens the company's future competitiveness. It's also one of Wong's responsibilities. As part of her job, she meets regularly with product developers, starting at the early design stage, when a new product is still just a sketch on a whiteboard. She asks the developers what information they plan to collect with the product, how they plan to use it, with whom the data will be shared, and how it will be kept secure. The issues are then discussed with Larry, Sergey, and Eric, and their recommendations are designed into the product.

One of the mandates is to inform users rigorously about how the information is used. When someone downloads Google's toolbar, they have to click on a box in order to allow PageRank to collect data about their surfing habits. If they do so, a privacy notice pops up to explain how the information is used, with a heading in bold red letters that says: "PLEASE READ CAREFULLY: IT'S NOT THE USUAL YADA YADA."

Larry and Sergey set the mandate that users must be provided with transparency—a clear explanation of what the company is up to—and the choice of whether or not to allow it. Even if the users decide they don't want their data collected, they can still download the toolbar without activating PageRank. That bucks the trend still prevalent for many Internet companies that says, essentially, "If you don't accept the terms then you can't use the product."

Similarly, when using Google's instant-messaging system, Google Talk, users can choose the option of going off the record, which prevents Google—and the people chatting—from keeping any record of the conversation.

Still, most people do not choose the privacy options, and Google keeps the data. But it has learned to compromise. Originally, Google did not put any limitation on the length of time it would keep the data. Privacy advocates complained, both to

Google and to government regulators. So, in 2007, Wong began a series of meetings with the product designers, asking them why they needed such data. The logs improve searches, spell-check features, and other services. But a big part of the reason they keep data, said the developers, was to ensure the security of the networks.

Any Internet company is subject to spam, fraud, and attacks known as "denial of service," in which a site is inundated with dozens of automatically generated requests in order to slow it down or make it crash. By keeping the data, Google can identify any patterns that led up to an attack and the computers used to instigate it, using the information to prevent similar future attacks.

"The fact of the matter is that the person successfully attacking us today has probably been trying for two years," says Wong. "So when we go back into the logs for a substantial amount of time, we're able to detect the pattern we have today. We can figure out all of the patterns we're seeing in an attack. We ask, 'What's the next step of this attack? What's the best way for us to try and stop it?' It is a historical record that helps us get to the answer that we need today."

Wong then asked the developers how long they actually needed to keep the data in order to maintain security. After collecting that feedback and reporting to Larry and Sergey, Google set its policy: it would keep the data for only eighteen months, "anonymizing" it after that so no individual or computer could be identified.

This placated no one. So Google engineers kept working on the problem to see if they could cut that retention time. The end result was that in 2008, Google announced that it would reduce the length of time data were kept by half, to nine months. "Our engineers said that they thought they could still get pretty good results, pretty good robustness, pretty good security, based on nine months," says Wong. "And I'll be really candid, we're giving up some quality, some ability to get really good search results faster, because we don't have that historical record. But we think we've built a system now, and improved our analytical tools, that will get us what we really, really need in nine months."

This presented another dilemma that forced Larry and Sergey to compromise. To them, user experience is of paramount importance, and the complaints about privacy were overblown. There has never been a documented case of Google violating its users' privacy, either losing control accidentally or engaging in such practices as selling information to spammers. Every complaint about Google falls into the category of what could happen, not what has happened. In general, Google has done a better job of protecting people's privacy than its competitors. In August 2005, the U.S. Department of Justice issued subpoenas to Google, America Online, Microsoft, and Yahoo to turn over two months' worth of search queries and all the URLs in their indexes, to aid in the Bush administration's defense of an Internet pornography law. Every company except Google quickly complied with the subpoenas. Google challenged it in court as a fishing expedition with no probable cause. In the end, Google managed to restrict the information to fifty thousand Web addresses, and did not have to turn over information on the key words users were using to search.

In fact, most Internet users worry about privacy less than they should and do little to protect themselves from it. But they do want the companies they deal with to provide the protection for them, and they rely on privacy advocates to force the issue on their behalf. The privacy advocates and government regulators raise the complaints with input from an extreme minority of users. This means that by cutting the data-retention time, Larry and Sergey accepted a compromise they feel is not really necessary, and sacrificed some of the user experience as a result, which can be seen as a violation of Google's promise to focus on the needs of its users.

Wong says that acceptance comes from the need to maintain the public trust. The public complaints from privacy advocates affect the overall public view of Google. "It's a tough balance," she says. "But if we don't do something to respect our users' privacy, that can be just as deadly as delivering a poor service. If the public thinks we're selfishly keeping data, that we're at risk of a hacking attack and all of this data is stored there, then we're going to lose their trust and they won't come no matter how good the service is."

That may still be a problem. Many privacy advocates, including the well-respected Electronic Frontier Foundation (EFF) and the European Union, still want Google to cut the retention time to six months. Wong says it's not possible without seriously compromising security and user experience.

Nevertheless, Wong says the company works well with organizations such as the EFF, where her point person is one of her former colleagues. All their recommendations are taken to the team, including Larry and Sergey, for discussion.

But a large number of complaints also come from people who express their opinions in the press without ever having spoken with Google or tried the products in question. Wong says she gets her fair share of complaints from people who don't really seem to want to solve problems, but "just want to cause a harangue." Some of the complaints are just crazy, and are dismissed with anger. One advocate, for example, called her and argued that Google should not retain any users' search histories at all, even though users frequently use them to find sites they've visited in the past that they want to visit again. The advocate's suggestion: users should just write down on paper the URLs of sites they've visited, keeping them safe from snooping eyes, or at least those who don't have access to their desk drawers.

Wong insists that Google is not just another company that creates a product and tosses it to the corporate attorneys to sign off on. "Privacy here is a concern for everyone, from our engineers to our executives. That's a really unique environment to work in. I don't think people always understand that aspect, or maybe they don't believe it, because there are certainly enough companies out there as a counterexample. But I believe it's true, and this is my group, so . . ." She trails off with a laugh.

Will these discussions continue as Google grows bigger and more powerful? If nothing else, Larry and Sergey will be forced to maintain this kind of structure to acknowledge and deal with complaints. If they compromise their ideals in the name of profit, they are likely to be less successful. Their ideals are what make Google stand out and engender trust from millions of people. Wong points out that when Google was young, it did not follow the example of other Internet companies, which regularly and deeply mined data about their users, sometimes selling the information to advertisers. "We didn't need to do that," she notes, "and we're wildly successful."

But on these issues, public perception is everything, and Google is struggling to convince users it's doing the right thing. Every move it makes as it grows more powerful is scrutinized and criticized. Telemarketers, spammers, and junk mailers have created huge skepticism about how any advertising megalith will use the data at its disposal, and there seems to be little Google can do about this.

Jim Barnett, the CEO of the online advertising firm Turn, sums up the sentiment: "The truth is that Google does care about user privacy and tries to be thoughtful about how it uses data. But they're also extremely competitive and are not bashful about trying to gain leverage in this competitive marketplace, which is what the DoubleClick acquisition was all about. It's a real concern. Google has extraordinary power in the online advertising space and the lion's share of search, and is growing every quarter. Advertisers are in the business of monetizing data, and Google has unique access to the data."

Trust as a Competitive Edge

Google's competitors are not bashful about trying to exploit those concerns. In late 2008, Microsoft and Yahoo announced their own promises to become better corporate citizens than Google when it came to privacy. Microsoft threw the ball in Google's court on December 8 by offering to cut the time it keeps user data to the EU-recommended six months—provided that Google and Yahoo did the same. Yahoo, which had the policy of retaining data for thirteen months, then took another shot on December 17 by saying it would cut retention time to just three months, except under limited circumstances. Ask was already offering a service that lets people opt out of any data retention, much as Google does when people download its toolbar option.

This now leaves Google looking like the bad guy, rather than the innovator trying to trim data retention as much as possible while minimizing the impact on the quality of its services. And it sets up a battle: which issue do users care more about—privacy or the quality of their searches?

These issues hurt. The "Don't be evil" company has rapidly risen to astounding name brand recognition and respect from consumers because of its policies. As Google gets bigger and as publicity over its policies spreads, its reputation is beginning to suffer, and its public stance against evil is becoming a liability.

Two organizations—TRUSTe, an online privacy advocate, and the Ponemon Institute, a think tank dedicated to privacy and data protection issues—have conducted an annual award for Most Trusted Company for Privacy since 2004. They survey more than six thousand U.S. consumers to collect opinions about which companies people feel are the most trustworthy and which do the best job of safeguarding personal information. From the beginning, Google consistently held the ranking as number ten or eleven on the list, except for two anomalies—2005 and 2008— when it dropped out of the top twenty altogether. In 2005 Google was getting a lot of publicity about its plans to enter the market in China. By contrast, Yahoo made it into the top twenty for the first time in 2008, into the fourteenth spot. Since Yahoo has had at least as many troubles as Google on the privacy and censorship front, the likely explanation is that supposedly non-evil Google gets vastly more publicity and criticism.

Fran Maier, CEO of TRUSTe, which monitors companies' online privacy policies and how well they're being enforced, acknowledges that the concern is largely fear of the unknown. "With Google, you have a company that pushes the envelope in a lot of different ways. They may be coming up with stuff that a lot of us have never seen before." Maier also emphasizes that while neither Microsoft nor Google made the top twenty, they are still "way up there" on the list. "A lot of people feel comfortable with both of them."

Larry Ponemon, the author of the study, told the *San Francisco Chronicle* that Google and Microsoft are suffering from "big company syndrome." Simply put, he said, "People figure that if you're big and collecting data, there must be an issue."

Google, it seems, is getting too big for the public's own good, and as a result, is increasingly seen as a bad wolf. Larry and Sergey do not like the idea of making goodwill gestures (e.g., cutting data retention time to three months) that they do not believe really serve their users' best interests. They assume that their logic will win out. This puts them in danger of losing the public relations war.

Google has more to lose than any of its competitors if it slips up. Such is the bane of anyone who publicly swears he will never be evil.

Chapter 9

The Ruthless Librarians

Everybody believes in something, and everybody, by virtue of the fact that they believe in something, uses that something to support their own existence.

—Frank Zappa

You can't create the world's greatest library without being a bit ruthless. In order to build the Library at Alexandria, the Ptolemies would confiscate all scrolls found on ships that entered the port of Alexandria, returning copies to the owners. They sent emissaries to every corner of the Mediterranean, the Middle East, and India to collect documents, bought or stolen. Legend has it that Ptolemy II brought Jewish scholars from all twelve tribes of Israel to translate the Torah into Greek, the preferred language of the region. Scholars also believe that the resulting text, the Septuagint, became the foundation of early Christians' understanding of the Old Testament. Even cookbooks were collected for the library. The Ptolemies also tried to collect the oldest version of every book they could, on the theory that those versions would be less corrupted by copying errors and later editors.

At that time, the Greeks were also adamant about preserving texts in their original form. Around 330 B.C., Athenian officials were disturbed to discover that actors were taking liberties with the works of Aeschylus, Sophocles, and Euripides, all dead for at least half a century and considered by Athenians to be the greatest writers who ever lived. So official versions of these works, as close to the originals as they could determine, were placed into the government's records office, and it was mandated by law that performers stick to the proper text.

A hundred years or so later, Ptolemy III decided he wanted the Library at Alexandria to possess the official versions of these plays from Athens, so he asked to borrow them to have them copied. To ensure their return, the Athenians made him pay an enormous deposit, the equivalent of millions of dollars today. But Ptolemy was greedier for great books than for money. He sent back the copies he had made instead, keeping the originals for the library and forfeiting his deposit. It was the biggest library fine ever paid. At least, until October 2008, when Google reached a settlement with book publishers.

L arry and Sergey have wanted to build an electronic library for books since they were at Stanford getting paid by the Digital Libraries Initiative. That concept was put on hold while they started up Google and focused on Web search, but it was never abandoned. The Internet does not have all the world's information, and almost none of the text that was created before 1995. But physical libraries are a rich storehouse of information created through the ages. Libraries are the obvious source to tap for books, since 95 percent of published works are now out of print. The largest libraries have spent decades or even hundreds of years building their collections, and some 75 percent of their inventory consists of books that are no longer being published, some of them very old. Sergey and Larry wanted to access that treasure every bit as much as the Ptolemy clan. The plan to realize that dream started coming together in 2002.

The first problem they had to face was how to get the books into digital form. They wondered how long it would take to scan and digitize every book in the world. So Larry decided to find out by scanning one book. He and Marissa Mayer, then a product manager, took a camera, a three-hundred-page book, and a metronome into his office. Using the metronome to keep time, Marissa turned the pages while Larry photographed each one. It took them forty minutes to capture all three hundred pages.

Larry and a small team then started visiting other book digitization projects, including one at his undergraduate alma mater, the University of Michigan. There he learned that the university estimated the time needed to digitize all seven million books it owned was one thousand years. He told University of Michigan president Mary Sue Coleman that Google could do it in six.

He also made what was then an unusual move for a software company by hiring robotics engineers to create a robotic page turner and scanner that could replace Marissa and Larry and their metronome. Such devices already existed on the market from other companies, but Larry thought that a good team at Google could do a better job by building a very gentle device that could handle older books with fragile pages. Software programmers at Google created a page-recognition software program that could recognize odd type sizes and unusual fonts in 430 different languages.

The team then started visiting large libraries to discuss their plan. At the Oxford University library, they examined centuries-old books that are stored carefully away and rarely brought out—and then only for qualified scholars. The Googlers talked enthusiastically about digitizing them and making them available to anyone. After more than a year of discussion, Oxford ended up becoming Google's first partner in the Google Print initiative (later renamed Google Book Search) with an agreement to digitize its collection of more than one million nineteenth-century books within three years.

The Publisher's Dilemma

That part was easy. Two-hundred-year-old books are no longer under copyright. But Larry also wanted more recent titles, some in print, some not. For this he needed the help of somebody who knew his way around the publishing business. He found a young man working at Random House named Adam Smith.

Smith is not your typical Google geek. Tall, thirtyish, athletically slim with neatly trimmed hair, he was loquacious on the day I met him, sporting the self-satisfied smile of someone who has been very successful and looking like the up-and-coming young publishing executive he once was. In 2003 Smith wrote an article in the *New York Times* about Random House's interest in going digital. It caught the attention of the boys at Google. In August of that year, he agreed to meet with Larry, corporate counsel David Drummond, and advertising executive Susan Wojcicki, who were going to be in New York in a couple of days. It wasn't to be a job interview, but Smith, a California native, hoped it would turn out that way. "I was thinking, this is my ticket back to California," he says.

The meeting did not come off as planned. The Googlers showed up in New York just as a huge blackout shut down Manhattan. Google called Smith in for a formal interview in November. That's when he finally met Larry.

As usual, the meeting was more of an information dump than an interview. "Larry was intellectually curious about the publishing industry, how it worked, and what motivated them. He wanted to know what drives them and what they're interested in. He wanted very much to get insight to the industry in a way I would call 'problem solving.' He said, 'Publishers must have problems, so what can we do for them? This is a big industry, and the Internet is going to be playing some role. So how can Google look at this from a product standpoint?'"

Larry was impressed enough with Smith's answers to hire him. Smith officially joined Google in December 2003. A year later Google announced its partnership to digitize the books of five libraries—those at Harvard, the University of Michigan,

Oxford, Stanford, and the New York Public Library. In each case, Google would cover all the expenses. It was important to the culmination of their long-standing desire to build the world's biggest library. "From their days at Stanford, Larry and Sergey never really gave up on their dream of digitizing books," says Smith.

The controversy started as soon as that initiative was announced. Officials at the French National Library immediately complained of bias. Just as the librarians of Alexandria heavily favored Greek volumes, the French complained that Google's program was biased in favor of English-language books. That controversy was quelled relatively easily. CEO Schmidt traveled to Paris to explain the program, and Google expanded it to foreign sources. This was Larry's intent from the start, his goals typically as ambitious as those of Ptolemy I. "We want all the world's books, in every language," says Smith. "And we want to be able to search across the full text of all books."

At first, they thought the idea of digitizing books would be easily palatable. For one thing, all publishers were watching the written word going digital and were struggling to find a way to join the revolution. "The industry was just coming off its first wave of ebook strategy," recalls Smith. "They didn't get the traction they were expecting. It wasn't clear that, left to their own devices, they would be able to make electronic books available to the public."

Smith and his team found a receptive audience. They met with major publishers and offered the same deal they had given the libraries: the publishers would supply the books, and Google would digitize them, put them online, make short excerpts available to the public, and provide links to sites where people could buy the books, if interested. Google would cover all expenses and wouldn't even collect any fees for referring buyers, although publishers could also run ads along with the displayed text, paying for clicks in a bidding auction like any other advertiser. In the case of books under copyright, people would be able to search through them to find a piece of information, but Google would provide only short snippets of text at a time. For publishers that wanted it, access would be further limited by restricting the amount of text available to just 20 percent of the book per month.

Google argued that the main benefit to publishers would be to raise the profile of books for sale. Most people don't want to read an entire book online, and would rather buy an easier-to-read paper version if they found the book interesting enough. Google's approach, says Smith, is to offer an experience that "is akin to walking into a bookstore and flipping through books."

In each publishing house, they found someone to champion Google's idea. Many of them said yes, some of them on a provisional basis, to see how well the program worked. Some balked at the concept that offering free access to books would cause people to buy them.

Google also makes the program available to anyone with a book for sale. Book authors can put searchable copies of their work on their blogs with a link to Amazon, collecting Amazon's 10 to 15 percent kickback every time someone clicks on the Amazon link and buys the books.

The program has been a success. Today it has digitized and posted about seven million books. Smith says that Google has found that the more book pages people view, the more likely they are to end up buying the whole book.

The Rest of the Books

But controversy over the program lingered. Books still in print were no problem. Books out of print were, because many of them are still under copyright, and the copyright owners are often difficult to find, especially when it comes to older published works.

Over the years, copyright law in the United States has become increasingly liberal toward the copyright owners. Modern copyright laws started a couple hundred years after Gutenberg invented the printing press in the fifteenth century. In 1662, Charles II, the king of Great Britain and Ireland, established the Licensing Act, creating a register of licensed books. This didn't protect the creators of the work, but provided a monopoly to the Stationer's Company to sell the works. In 1709, under the reign of Queen Anne, Britain established the first true copyright, known as the Statute of Anne. That act granted exclusive rights for twenty-one years, but this time to the authors instead of the publishers. Since then, copyright laws have been an issue of great controversy, revision, and debate.

In the United States, the founding fathers granted Congress

the right to set copyright laws in the Constitution. Congress did so in 1790, stipulating that copyright holders should hold the rights to their works for fourteen years and had the right to renew once for a second fourteen-year term. After that, the works were in the public domain. Since then, the length of copyright has been repeatedly expanded. In 1831 it was extended to twenty-eight years with a fourteen-year renewal. In 1909 the renewal term was also expanded, to twenty-eight years. In 1976 it was expanded to the life of the creator of the work plus fifty years. In 1998 it grew to seventy years after the death of the work's creator. This was later extended to ninety-five years. By this time, it became diffi-cult to find just who owned the copyright, especially for obscure and out-of-print works. And copyrights have been applied to more and more types of works, including photographs, film, music, dra-matic compositions, and eventually all published works, includ-ing computer programs, semiconductor chips, and online works. Nobody has to apply for copyright anymore—their works' mere publication gives them all rights automatically.

Stanford professor and legal scholar Lawrence Lessig, who has advised Larry and Sergey on the matter, argues that this is unreasonable and that copyright laws have reached onerous levels that do more harm than good. He points out that in 1930, 10,027 books were published, and that 9,853 are now out of print, put-ting them out of reach of the public. But it's almost impossible to determine which heirs, descendants, or corporations own the copyright to the vast majority of those books, which prevents them from being republished. Google, Lessig says, is trying to bring these books back to life. "Publishers don't have a moral position to stand on," he says. He describes Google Print this way: "The project promises to radically enhance our access to the past—to remind us of forgotten information. It is the greatest gift to knowledge since, well, Google."

The big problem with current copyright law, Lessig argues, is that people can no longer create derivative works, a long-standing approach to creating new work. Shakespeare's works are repeatedly used as inspiration, such as for the Broadway musical *West Side Story,* a retelling of *Romeo and Juliet.* Disney has been a powerful force in lobbying for extended copyright, preventing anyone from reproducing Mickey Mouse or creating a derivative character. Ironically, Mickey Mouse was itself a derivative work. The first Mickey cartoon, *Steamboat Willie*, from 1928, was itself a parody of a Buster Keaton movie, *Steamboat Bill, Jr.,* which was created the same year—despite the fact that U.S. copyrights were extended to films in 1912.

Book publishers have a problem with Google's ambitions to index all the world's books. Google promised that it would respect any copyright, as long as it could figure out who held it. There is no comprehensive registry of copyright, but the copyright owner could come forward and claim the work, subjecting it to the same terms as works still in print. This wasn't good enough for publishers. On October 19, 2005, the Authors Guild and the Association of American Publishers, the latter representing five major publishers—including Penguin Group (USA) Inc., the parent company of the publisher of this book—filed a lawsuit against Google, arguing that the plan to digitize, search, and show snippets of copyrighted books was illegal. The argument was that Google should find the copyright holders themselves, a task that Google said would be prohibitively expensive.

Google's view has been that the Online Copyright Infringement Liability Limitation Act of 1997, which became Title II of the Digital Millennium Copyright Act of 1996, protects its efforts, since the act states that online publishers are obligated to remove copyrighted material only after copyright owners ask them to do so. But many experts disagree with this view, insisting that it applies only to sites where users post copyrighted works on a site owned by someone else, such as YouTube.

At Google's annual shareholders meeting in 2004, Google lawyer David Drummond said, "We do run into a lot of areas where our innovation bumps up against laws that were not designed for the world we now live in. Sometimes others don't share our commitment [to change]. Trademark and copyright laws are two areas where we have legitimate disagreements [with existing companies and lawmakers]."

In October 2005, Eric Schmidt wrote an op-ed piece in the *Wall Street Journal* titled "Books of Revelation." In it, he argued that for most books, the amount of information available through Google Book Search would be comparable to a library card catalog. The lawsuit by the publishers would keep 60 percent of existing books out of Google's library. "We find it difficult to believe that authors will stop writing books because Google Print makes them easier to find, or that publishers will stop selling books because Google Print might increase their sales," wrote Schmidt.[1] He argued that book sales would increase and that people in developing countries would have access to information they could not possibly get any other way.

Larry and Sergey see their task as nothing less than creating a new Hellenistic Age. "We did not think necessarily we could make money" off Book Search, says Sergey. "We just feel this is part of our core mission. There is fantastic information in books. Often when I do a search, what is in a book is miles ahead of what I find on a Web site."[2]

This Time, Compromise

But Larry and Sergey are getting older, and they have developed more willingness to compromise—some say they are compromising their idealism. On October 28, 2008, they reached a settlement with the publishers over Google Book Search. In exchange for the right to provide free full-text versions of out-of-print books, it agreed to make payments totaling $125 million. The money, which comes from revenue Google generates from publishing the works, goes to authors and publishers. It has also agreed to create a not-for-profit Books Rights Registry to try to locate the copyright holders, to collect and maintain details of their rights, and provide a way for the copyright holders to request inclusion in or exclusion from the project. "The boys have grown up," says Schmidt. "The young men I started with seven years ago are now seasoned executives. They're no longer the stereotype [of computer geeks]. It's offensive to them to treat them any other way."

David Drummond was the one who worked out the settlement. But Larry, Sergey, and Schmidt all signed on immediately. "When David came in and briefed us, it was a no-brainer," says Schmidt. "There was never any significant dissent. It was a clever and innovative approach to the problem. We have to pick our battles." And, one might note, $125 million is no longer a prohibitive amount of money to Google in exchange for ending a costly and time-consuming lawsuit (despite its pared-down daycare system).

Sergey enthusiastically praised the settlement when it was announced. "Google's mission is to organize the world's information and make it universally accessible and useful. Today, together with the authors, publishers, and libraries, we have been able to make a great leap in this endeavor. While this agreement is a real win-win for all of us, the real victors are all the readers. The tremendous wealth of knowledge that lies within the books of the world will now be at their fingertips."

Some people, however, do want Larry and Sergey to remain the idealistic geeks defending their causes. Criticism of the settlement came from online. Some bloggers complained that by selling out instead of pursuing the case in court, Google gave up the opportunity to establish the legality of providing short passages from published works, which should fall under the "fair use" provisions of copyright laws. And, in fact, Larry and Sergey still believe that they are covered by fair use laws, even without the settlement. "The agreement we came to was not about lack of confidence in the legal case," says Smith, "but about what we and publishers could do together." The prevailing view at Google is that the settlement serves the interests of all parties involved. In response to the criticism over the settlement, Smith says, "Google isn't in the business of establishing legal precedents."

What About the Future?

Further into the future, the problem becomes even more complex. As technology improves, it will become easier to read entire digitized books online or through specially designed digital book readers. As books are digitized, it will be easy for pirates to copy and share them. People are used to lending books to friends, and electronic publishing will make it possible to share books with a few million of them. And given the nature of the Internet, people are likely to create book "mashups," combining excerpts from many different books, videos, and music into new works. Who collects revenue from such projects?

Google does not create the problem, it simply adds fuel to the fire of a trend that has already been made inevitable by the Internet. When there are pirated books and mashups floating about the Internet, Google's search engine will find them.

Existing industries still have to figure out how to deal with the Internet and its changes. The Internet, with Google pushing it along, is simply and significantly a new alternative to existing forms of media and entertainment. Bloggers, for example, have become a huge form of publishing. Social networks pull young people away from older forms of entertainment and socializing. Google has figured out how to make money off all these new forms of entertainment, while every competitor is struggling with that issue.

Online news is rapidly replacing the local newspaper. Google and companies such as Craigslist are providing a better and more cost-effective form of classified advertising, eating up a huge portion of newspapers' revenue. Many news publishers don't like this fact. Belgian news companies have successfully sued Google just for offering snippets of their articles before sending readers off to the source for the full story.

All publishers will have to come to terms with the Internet and will need to be deeply involved in the coming changes, including figuring out how to make a buck in an age of rampant piracy—or they could be sideswiped by these rapidly moving vehicles of change.

Most likely, Google will play a huge role in the transformation of these industries, and publishers and creators will have to follow its lead. Their best bet is to start thinking more like Larry and Sergey. They need to create economic models that accept a certain level of piracy. The best way to do that is to figure out how to serve the needs of their customers, rather than suing them to keep them from sharing works through the Internet. Google has already begun experimenting with, and tracking, the value of free distribution as a marketing tool.

But the solutions to these problems will not come easily, and many of the answers will be determined in court, often with Google as a defendant. It is likely that the supreme courts of many countries will end up defining the rights of publishers and, perhaps, redefining the scope of copyright law. The difference is that Larry and Sergey may not fight as hard to defend their views. They're becoming less ruthless than the Ptolemy clan.

Chapter 10

The Google Cloud

It's best to do one thing really, really well.

> —Number two on the list of "Ten things Google has found to be true" on the corporate Web site

To punish me for my contempt for authority, fate made me an authority myself.

> —Albert Einstein

Larry and Sergey have always insisted that Google is a search company. Any assertion that it is becoming a media company or a PC company or a hardware company is dismissed as fantasy. The response is, according to Google spokesman David Krane, "We do search. But we reserve the right to define search any way we want."

Really? Do PC applications, e-mail, cell phone operating

systems, Web browsers, Wiki information sites, social networks, and photo editing sites really fall into the category of "search"? Pundits and competitors have criticized Google for stepping far beyond the boundaries of its core mission in an attempt to take over the entire computing industry. In fact, Google used to say that it focused on search but let its engineers and computer scientists dabble in whatever they wanted with 20 percent of their time. Now the company says that 70 percent of its research is focused on its core competency of search, 20 percent is dedicated to related products that include search elements, and 10 percent is anything else.

But there is logic behind most of the company's seemingly scattershot approach to diversification. Put at the top of the list "Because they can."

Larry and Sergey understand the Internet, and they know how to use it. In the year 2000, when pundits and publications were declaring the death of the Internet, Larry and Sergey understood its enormous potential. The Internet has made computers and communications astoundingly more efficient and less costly. When Larry and Sergey built Google's computing infrastructure to handle rapid searches, they realized it could do so much more.

That infrastructure is too big to be contained in any one building—or any one city, for that matter. On the Internet, Google links millions of small computers into hordes that can speedily make their calculations for people in their region and speed the results back without having to travel halfway around the planet. Sometimes a single task is split among several computers that do the job in tandem, operating as a single computer. That's the main reason Larry and Sergey decided to buy up miles of fiber optic cables at fire sale prices. This vision of massively parallel computing was articulated in the late 1990s by venture capitalists and other dot-com companies, but it took the vision of Larry and Sergey to make it happen. They didn't just build a huge network to move information along quickly, they also created a new kind of supercomputer, one whose brain is scattered throughout the world, connected by fiber optic nerves that make it function as a single entity. It's a network supercomputer.

Google's supernetwork is by far the largest and most powerful network of computers in the world. It's located in "server farms" scattered throughout the world—from Atlanta to China to Zurich—and it's growing every day. One of the largest server farms is located in the town of The Dalles, Oregon, near sources of cheap hydroelectric power and a surplus of fiber optic cables. Called "Project 02," the farm is the size of two football fields and has cooling towers four stories high.

The number of computers Google has installed is a closely guarded secret. When the company was just a couple of years old, Sergey revealed that the number was "over ten thousand," and that's still the number Google uses when asked. But the research firm Gartner Group has made an estimate based on the amount of money Google spends on computer equipment each year, and puts the total at more than one million.

These servers include load balancers, to move work from busy or broken computers to others that can handle the work; proxy servers, which store data temporarily and filter things such as spam; Web servers, which find search results; data gathering servers, which index Web pages; ad servers, to pick out relevant ads; and even spelling servers, which suggest alternate spellings of search terms.

Just as Larry and Sergey built their own network to run their search engine at Stanford, they designed a unique network when Google was young. And, just as they did at Stanford, they built it from the cheapest PCs they could get—commodity PCs running on Intel chips, running the open operating system Linux. They don't buy the latest, most powerful generation of PCs for the network. They calculate which recent generation of PCs gives the most computing power per dollar.

Being PCs, the machines regularly fail. Because of the design of the system, that (usually) doesn't bring down any part of the system. The work is automatically transferred to other PCs until the errant machines are pulled out of the system and replaced with new ones. Sometimes, however, too many may fail or a part of the network goes down, shutting down access to e-mail or documents or other services, causing havoc, and eliciting widespread complaints from the people who rely on them. This is the biggest potential problem in Google's vision of network computing. Google crashes are infrequent compared to those of most systems, but many more people are affected by them.

This supernetwork is an enormous distributed supercomputer. Anybody who uses an application from Google is tapping into this incredible store of computing power. This is the main reason Google's competitors have such a hard time matching the company's capabilities. And it allows Google to enter any business that Larry, Sergey, or their ambitious team of computer scientists and engineers finds interesting.

The Idea Machine

Google is using this power to change the rules of business, from news delivery to PC computing to books to watching videos. No wonder many business executives are—or if they aren't, should be—afraid of this new giant on the block. If Larry and Sergey get their way, it will be extraordinarily difficult for traditional businesses to compete as they have since the start of the twentieth century. Any business that deals in the collection or dissemination of information is in danger of having its infrastructure collapse beneath its feet like Wile E. Coyote standing on an overhanging bluff. Larry and Sergey move like roadrunners, charging ahead with their visionary plans, saying nothing about where they're headed, or why.

There's a good reason for that. They often don't know where they're going until they get there.

Google is an idea machine. Some of the ideas come from the top. Larry, for example, thought of the idea for "street views" in Google Maps—that is, actual photographs of the streets and buildings to help people identify their destinations—before Google Maps was even created. But this is not Apple, and Larry and Sergey are not Steve Jobs. The company is not centrally controlled, and ideas can come from anywhere.

The problem with most corporations is that it's hard to get people to think differently. People are more likely to think incrementally rather than boldly. Many tech companies deal with this problem by creating formalized "skunk works," specialized teams put together to work on an innovative new idea. At Google, everyone is a skunk. Google's innovation machine is designed to create hundreds or thousands of research projects, many of them one-person teams. That's the idea behind the concept of 20 percent time, which allows scientists and engineers at the company to spend up to one day a week working on their own ideas.

At a Technology, Entertainment, Design (TED) conference for big thinkers in these fields a few years ago, Larry explained how it came about. "Both Sergey and I went to Montessori schools. For some reason this has been incorporated into Google. We've embodied this as the 20 percent time. For 20 percent of your time you can do what you think is important to do. . . . After all, Mendel discovered the laws of genetics as a hobby. As companies get bigger they find it harder to have small innovative projects. We had that problem too for a while. And we said, 'Oh, we really need a new concept.' "

Not every engineer has new ideas to pursue, and not everyone takes that time. Some may join up with other people's projects. Some may use the time to take classes. Some may formally set aside one day per week for a project, while others may occasionally dabble. All that's required is letting their managers know what they want to do. "We're flexible," says senior vice-president Alan Eustace. "You have to have ways to set aside the time when you need to. Otherwise the upstream stuff isn't going to happen."

The process goes beyond giving researchers the ability to take time off from their regular jobs. Ideas are shared, discussed, analyzed, and criticized. To make that happen, Google has created a database of information about every project every engineer is working on. All the engineers in the company have access to the database and can find out what anyone else is doing. Any engineer can examine the design documents of any project, add comments about the projects, and e-mail members of teams to offer comments and opinions. They can even rate other people's comments. In engineering, everyone is a critic.

Larry and Sergey created that system to prevent ideas from dying before they ever get past the concept stage. "Where most companies fail on innovation is that they don't take into account the whole pipeline of innovation," says Eustace. "They tend to have a suggestion box mentality. Next week maybe somebody will empty the box. You can't really get feedback on your ideas, and they die on the vine. We have a lot of different ways to get feedback."

But they also have to withstand the scrutiny of Larry and Sergey if they think it has commercial potential. The founders decide where the company will go next. And they are ruthless judges of product designs. The product designers and engineers schedule meetings with Sergey and Larry to report on progress, and the pair does not soft-pedal their critiques. CEO Eric Schmidt describes them as "brutal."

Tough Critics

Although Schmidt's role is to run the business and focus on growing the company, he defers to Larry and Sergey's judgment about which technology and products will get them there. But it's not always a harmonious meeting of the minds. "There were times when Larry and Sergey would do things I was very unhappy about because they were so precocious," he says. Their arguments were often heated, and Schmidt decided that it was a bad idea to conduct them publicly. "Eventually we agreed that we would have an argument privately," he says.

The argument that led to the private meetings came a few years ago, when the company had to decide which browser Google should focus on when designing products. Microsoft's Internet Explorer has the overwhelming market share, but technology-savvy Interneters such as Larry and Sergey favor the more elegant and open Firefox browser from Mozilla.org, a nonprofit group that allows the geeky public to design new features. As an open system, it's easier for outsiders to create add-on programs that users can choose to add or not. Some Web sites will only work properly and fully with Internet Explorer.

A meeting was scheduled to include Larry, Sergey, Schmidt, and Google engineers to make the decision. Sergey arrived late to the meeting, and it started late. When he arrived, he hated the approach the team was favoring. "Sergey throws up all over the decision in front of everybody," recalls Schmidt. "I said, 'Stop! Everyone leave the room.' I sat down and told them, don't do that. If we're going to have an argument, let's have it in private."

In that meeting, Schmidt told Sergey, "I'm willing to do what you want, although I don't agree with it." But he told Larry and Sergey they had to come to an agreement on the issue, and gave them until 6:00 P.M. the following day to do so. Then he left the room to let them fight it out. "This was a test to see what would happen," says Schmidt.

What happened was not what he expected. The next day, the deadline passed with no answer. So Schmidt went to Larry and Sergey to get one. Their response: "Well, we gave the team a new set of assignments, and we're meeting again tomorrow. We came up with a completely new approach."

The following day, after feedback from the engineers, Larry and Sergey agreed on the new approach. They had come up with a way to reengineer the development process so that the programs would work with any browser. The issue was now moot. "All the team was happy and I learned something," says Schmidt. "I didn't need to decide the answer. I just needed to make sure all the ambiguities were exposed and that the right people were in the room to get it set up. Sometimes there's a better answer that's not in the current solution set. Had we stopped and just done what Sergey wanted or just done what I'd approved we would not have gotten to the better algorithm."

This realization was a real mind-opener to Schmidt. "It helped me understand my role," he says. "Now I try not to make important decisions unless they're really important ones. Rather, I've tried to make the culture work. The way it feels to me is they are smarter, quicker, more opinionated and earlier than I am. They're on an issue earlier than I am. My job is to make sure that reality and what we're doing match together for a positive outcome."

Schmidt still operates on that principle today. At the time I met with him in November 2008, he had just come from another debate, although a much milder one this time, with Larry. (Sergey was out of town.) Larry had long believed that there was incredible opportunity for creating applications for mobile phones. Schmidt was ready to bag that market for a while. So he met with Larry and told him that despite all the applications Google and others had built for cell phones, "there's not anything incredible."

So Larry pointed out one such application and told Schmidt about all the opportunities it represented for the future. Schmidt was impressed with his thinking and scheduled a meeting for the following day to discuss the potential. "The meeting happened because Larry and I were thinking similarly, but he was thinking with better specificity. I was just generally complaining."

That's a big part of the reason that the number of services Google offers grows constantly. Although management insists that it's still primarily a search company, outsiders, including Wall Street analysts, see what appears to be a scattershot diversification. There are, however, specific targets in mind. Larry and Sergey are focused on all the possibilities of the Internet, and many others besides. Many of their efforts are designed to fill in spaces they feel are not being filled properly, and they're very fond of showing others what they believe is the right approach. Says

Stanford president and Google board member John Hennessy, "Larry and Sergey have very broad and eclectic interests."

Those interests are especially strong when it comes to getting people online so they can use Google's services, and coming up with new ways to gather information for people to search through, from e-mail to news to people's own documents.

The Media Biz

Increasingly, Google is looking like a media company. In 2006 it paid $1.6 billion to buy YouTube, the world's leading supplier of online video. People post homemade videos, pieces of television programs, TV commercials, and anything else that strikes their fancy. But that's the key difference between Google and a traditional media company. Google does not create its own video content. It merely provides the means for others to create content and distribute it through Google's services. It's another effort to build the world's greatest online library.

Nevertheless, YouTube has gotten Google into a cauldron of trouble. Soon after Google bought YouTube in 2006, Viacom filed a $1 billion lawsuit against YouTube and Google for allowing users to post copyright-protected videos on the site.

That suit is still crawling through the courts. In October 2008, Viacom issued a statement that said, essentially, if Google can settle with book publishers, it can do the same with Hollywood. "Copyright laws provide creators with the incentive to create the works consumers crave," said the statement. "It is unfortunate that the publishers had to spend years, and millions of dollars, for Google to honor that principle. We hope that Google avoids the wasted effort and comes more quickly to respect movies and television programming."

These days, such videos regularly disappear as soon as they're posted, as Google complies with demands from the programs' producers. But just as quickly, they reappear, posted by someone else. It's an ongoing battle, in which Larry and Sergey firmly believe they are protected by the Digital Millennium Copyright Act of 1996, which says that Internet service providers (ISPs) are not liable for illegal postings by others using their services, as long as the operators remove infringing content and do not induce users to upload those postings.

So why get involved in video distribution in the first place? There are two reasons. For one, it's a huge business that promises to give Google more places to park ads. The other is that it really does affect Google's ability to improve search.

Google does not have access to all the world's information—yet. Just as they want to digitize books so people can search through them, Larry and Sergey want to ensure that there is a large pool of video content to search through, too. That is not an easy task. The future of search is much more complex, more three-dimensional. It involves the ability to search through images, sound, music, time, and space. Google is experimenting with ways to parse any type of information so that it can be recognized and found. The easiest approach, searching through the labels applied to pictures and sounds, is extremely limited.

Google needs to be able to capture words, recognize their meaning, and put them into the search index.

This is also the reason Google bought Picasa, a picture-sharing site that also allows people to edit and manipulate their photos. Its research is still secret, but many other researchers are experimenting with techniques to automatically search for and identify photographs. At Stanford, researchers have been trying to identify the content of photographs by recognizing whether they include faces, or the blue skies and green grass of landscapes. Today's cameras also capture the dates and times that images were taken, and one day it may even be possible to use global positioning satellites to determine where a picture was taken. Through Picasa, Google will have access to that data.

It's also very important that Google can observe how people use different types of information. Everything someone posts online says something about him: his interests, opinions, likes and dislikes. By integrating people's data from many different sources, Google's computers collect what's known as metadata, a powerful tool for improving its products and presence on the Internet.

The PC Biz

Metadata can come from almost anywhere. While they're at it, how about adding everyone's personal content to the Internet? This means e-mails, spreadsheets, documents, and other products of individual creativity. The goal is primarily to make each individual's information available to her, to keep it from unwanted prying eyes and ears, but also to share it if she wishes. Every piece of data says something about the individual using it, allowing Google to further customize searches to that individual's needs. And if people are using Google products to create that information, it's easier for the company to analyze it, categorize it, and add it to the reams of metadata it has access to. When people use Google's applications programs, such as Google Docs, the company has free access to the information (although it promises to use that info only for the creator's benefit).

This category also pits Google against one of the most powerful technology companies of all time. Microsoft sees Google as an infiltrator into its core business, and is trying to respond in kind. The two companies have started an aggressive dance around each other's business. So far, Google is steadily gaining ground on Microsoft, whose efforts to have an impact on search and online advertising can best be described as luke-cold.

It's easy to say that Google is entering Microsoft's business in order to counterattack Redmond's forays into search and advertising. There is some truth to that, although Google executives all deny it, sometimes credibly. Says Dave Girouard, who heads Google's applications business, "It's not in the DNA of Google. Not that we're not competitive, but I don't think people at Google would ever see this as going after Microsoft. But it's a pleasant side effect."

But there is another temptation Larry and Sergey cannot resist. The computer industry is once again cracking at the seams, showing its inefficiencies and becoming too expensive—just as it did at the end of the mainframe era. Companies such as Google, Salesforce, and Zoho, a division of software company AdventNet Inc., are using the Internet to make computing more efficient, more powerful, and cheaper. The programs and data no longer reside in the PC, but online—in Google's case, as part of its supernetwork. People tap into these applications through the Internet. The Internet is becoming the computer.

This trend is known as "software as a service" (SaaS) or "cloud computing." Software is not sold and installed in personal computers; it's run online in the amorphous Internet cloud, and rented or given away to users. The data can also be stored in the cloud.

It's a reversal of the trend that Bill Gates exploited to make Microsoft famous. Before the invention of the microprocessor, only corporations could afford computers. The work was done on large mainframes that employees tapped into through private networks. But mainframes and their networks were easily overloaded if too many people tried to use them at once. After Intel invented the microprocessor in the late 1970s, putting most of the brains of a computer (albeit a very small one) onto a desktop PC, people no longer needed to rely on infinitely more expensive mainframes.

The Internet offers a huge benefit to even simple computing. Today, PCs are relatively expensive. A decently equipped new computer starts at about $1,000. They become obsolete after a few years. Adding too many applications causes internal communications problems as different programs try to access the same channels. Memory chips get full and slow down. People end up trashing them for a new generation of computers with better processors, more memory, and even bigger and more complex software. They spend another $1,000.

But imagine a PC designed for cloud computing. The software runs on Google's supernetwork, so the PC does not need the latest microprocessors. The data is stored in the cloud, so the PC does not need the most expensive memory chips. The software is automatically updated, debugged, and improved remotely by Google. Under this scenario, PCs become much cheaper; the software, free (as long as you're willing to live with a few ads); and obsolescence is slowed immensely. Fully realizing this vision will take some time, because it requires constant access to high-speed Internet connections that do not crash.

But for years Internet bloggers and analysts have repeated rumors that Google is creating its own PC operating system. It's generally seen as an unwise attempt to undercut Microsoft. But it would also increase Google's presence in our lives, and its access to our data, enormously. It makes sense for Google to do it.

Several bloggers have speculated that Google could adapt its Android smartphone operating system specifically for PCs and team up with PC makers to create the hardware. Some companies are already pushing the idea. A Motorola spinoff called Freescale recently announced it is developing a chipset to run

Google's Android smartphone operating system on "netbooks." These pared-down $200 notebook computers, designed for Web surfing, are rapidly becoming the next major trend in computing. And a company called Quickoffice has announced it is creating software that will allow people to view Microsoft Word, Excel, and PowerPoint applications on their Android phones.

Google has even teamed up with Microsoft to take on Apple's iPhone. It's using Microsoft's ActiveSync technology for a new utility called Google Sync, which allows people to synchronize their data from Google Calendar and Google Contact over the air with their iPhone. Apple charges $100 a year for that service.

On a lesser scale, rumors have discussed a supposed secret project within Google code-named Platypus, also known as the GDrive. Leaked documents indicate that Google is trying the system internally. GDrive is more than a memory device. Users can upload the entire contents of their computer to Google's cloud, including all the data and software applications they use. Whenever that person is online, everything is automatically synchronized. Any data added either to the PC or the cloud is updated on the other device as well. The big advantage is this: you can drop your computer in the bathtub and completely destroy it, a disaster for most people. But with this system, you merely buy a new computer, connect to your personal GDrive with your password, and your old computer is reborn in a new shell.

Google denies all rumors, right up until the time it announces a product. For years there were rumors that Google was getting into the phone business with its own smartphone. Technically, the rumors were not quite accurate. Google created an operating system to control a cell phone, and in late 2008, cell phone manufacturer HTC announced it was building the hardware, while T-Mobile announced that the phone would work on its cellular network.

Google has already created a lesser version of the GDrive, a product called Google Gears. This program does not copy an entire PC, but it does copy all the documents users create, either on their PCs or online using Google Docs. When new documents are created or updated, the system is supposed to automatically update those documents either on the PC or online. It's still buggy, though, and does not update reliably.

Not all the products these days are created in-house. Increasingly, Google is buying promising small companies with good ideas, a presence in a business Google covets, or technology that can enhance its own products. Google has acquired more than fifty companies to fill those needs, including blogging services, photo sharing and editing programs, e-mail, Maps, Google Earth, Web browsers, mobile phone applications, and analytical software to help run a business.

A recent article in *Forbes* magazine put it well. Google's goal is to leverage the vast resources of the Internet to put together "little bits on an unimaginable scale." With that approach, Google is unquestionably displacing Microsoft as the center of the computer industry. Microsoft's model is PC-centric, while Google's is Internet-centric.

There is, of course, room both for PCs operating independently and for cloud computing, but Microsoft places the emphasis on the former, with the Internet as a peripheral system, while to Google, the cloud is the computer. There are merits to both approaches. Microsoft's is more expensive for consumers, while Google's has a higher risk of network crashes shutting down access to one's programs and data.

More Microsoft Mischief

Google executives have long said that they are not trying to compete directly with Microsoft. "We try not to focus on what they [Microsoft] are doing," says Larry. But it seems to work out that way. In February 2007, Google moved from being primarily a consumer products company to entering the enterprise software field, creating products for corporations, a field now dominated by Microsoft. Salesforce.com has pointed the way with a cloud computing system that displaces corporate software from Oracle, normally run on company mainframes or mini-computers. Google's group is headed by David Girouard, president of the enterprise business and Google Applications. A Dartmouth grad in computer engineering with an MBA from the University of Michigan, Girouard has been a consultant with business consulting firms Booz Allen and Accenture, an executive at Apple, and an entrepreneur. He joined Google in 2004. He says that putting Google's software into corporations and getting them to run programs online is another way to collect all the world's information, although this information is in the restricted access section of the Internet library, available only to the corporations that own it. "A lot of the world's information is in e-mail, in filing cabinets, in the workplace. It's an acute part of what limits people's access to information. Web content per se was never how we defined ourselves."

Microsoft became an enterprise computer company by sneaking in the back door. Corporate IT departments were reluctant to switch from a centrally controlled mainframe system to a distributed system of PCs that individuals owned, used, and upgraded themselves. But PCs became cheap enough for managers to buy with a corporate credit card, and they spread to the extent that IT departments had to accept and integrate them into the corporate systems. Girouard is infiltrating corporations with the same tactic. "What Internet technology is used in every business?" he asks. "Google.com. Web search. The job of my organization is to transform cloud computing into something that corporate IT does care about and makes use of. It's a rogue approach to changing corporate computing."

Microsoft's desktop PC programs still dominate in corporations. But Girouard says Google is making substantial progress, and that there are more than ten million business users of its applications programs—both free ad-supported versions and paid versions more appropriate to corporations. Half a million businesses have signed up for the paid versions, with more than three thousand more signing up every day. Most are small businesses, but a few are big companies, including Genentech, Procter & Gamble, and General Electric. Virtually all the companies, however, are still using Microsoft applications as well. "We view this as a marathon, not a sprint," says Girouard.

Microsoft's view is a remnant of founder Bill Gates's vision, stuck in the old model he helped create. Like the mainframers—including IBM—that Microsoft helped displace from the center of the computing world, Microsoft finds it hard to completely displace its older, more expensive model. IBM had trouble weaning itself from its expensive mainframes, and Microsoft has trouble extricating itself from its more costly PC software model. Selling software is Microsoft's money maker. In order to compete with Google, it will have to learn to make money from leasing out software, adopting free or cheap open systems such as Linux, and generating revenue from online advertising, where it has consistently failed. "The trajectory in computer science is clearly on our side," says Girouard.

Bill Gates, in fact, had trouble accepting the power of the Internet. Before 1995, Microsoft was trying to create its own "information superhighway," a proprietary networking system that it alone would own and control. In 1996, I conducted an extensive interview with then-CEO Gates, who was still angrily dismissing the future power of the Internet. "Oh, sure, the Internet is everything," he sneered. The PC visionary had trouble looking beyond his own bubble.

At Google, any idea is fair game. "Most people would like to divide the world in certain ways—enterprise products, consumer products, media," says Girouard. "Larry and Sergey don't see things that way. They see people and the way people use technology. They ask, 'What problems are people having that brave, smart computer scientists can help with?' They never assess whether we have the DNA to do it right. They just look for hard problems to solve that would have a material effect on millions of people."

Not everything works, and Google has killed a lot of projects. In December 2008, as recession put pressure on even Google's bottom line, Larry decided to kill a lot of projects that seemed to be going nowhere or were not successfully competing with existing products from other companies. The company ceased work on Dodgeball, a mobile social networking service, and Jaiku, a Twitter-like microblogging service. And it killed Mashup Editor, a product in private testing that allowed outsiders to create new Web applications using Google services and technologies.

Some projects have been killed by more successful and ambitious offerings within Google. One is Google Video, which was made obsolete by YouTube. Google Catalog Search fell victim to Google Book Search. Part of being innovative means being willing to fail. But it also means being able to succeed, and Google's list of new products and new industries to tackle keeps growing.

Even re-creating products already invented by others, Google benefits from the ability to collect more data when people use Google's version. Google's new Chrome browser, for example, has the potential to increase Google's knowledge of what sites people are visiting. It has its own RSS reader—a software product that allows people to automatically collect feeds from news sources and bloggers—even though other companies already have perfectly good RSS feed products. But it allows Google to collect still more data about people's habits on the Internet and apply it to their computer algorithms.

Google executives tend to argue that the existing products, especially those created by Microsoft, are in dire need of improvement. "These apps are coming into a market owned by apps that are now twenty to thirty years old," says Girouard. "It's clearly the case that we have crazy new apps; that the fit and polish is not there. It's breakthrough technology, but the degree of fit and polish, we will work on."

As for tolerating a string of failures, most good companies in Silicon Valley know that you cannot innovate without being willing to make mistakes. And people tend to forget that Bill Gates built an empire on me-too products, most of which seemed like failures for years until the company got it right. Even Microsoft's operating system was a derivative of one created by another company, which Microsoft licensed from it. Many of the major software applications Microsoft created were based on products invented elsewhere. And, like Microsoft, Google is wealthy enough to spend the money on experimentation.

A more substantive criticism may be that Larry and Sergey have a tendency to believe that they can do a better job than any competitor, creating many things that they could just as well buy. Google's supernetwork is an example. Although it's built with off-the-shelf PCs, their design is modified for efficiency, as is the network connecting them. But does Google really need to invent everything anew?

One thing Larry and Sergey have trouble with is figuring out how to complete a product. Their computer scientist approach is to release products before they're perfected, using the Internet to collect opinions from millions of users to tweak the design. In general, it's a brilliant approach, something that could not be done as efficiently before the Internet. And it's a huge contrast to Microsoft, which creates its products behind closed laboratory doors and releases products that are too complicated for most people to fully exploit. Bill Gates has admitted that this ends up being the case because Microsoft relies on "experts," mainly product reviewers, to design products. Every product reviewer makes a list of features that a product should have, and creates tables checking off the items on the list and comparing which products have the most check marks. And every reviewer has a different list.

Google's products invariably start off with lousy reviews because of everything they lack compared with the competition. But the company carefully adds features that are really needed by most users, and ends up with a clean, easy-to-use product, if not the most versatile. The Gmail program, for example, was panned by a lot of reviewers when it first came out. It's now widely respected for its simplicity and dependence on Google's search capabilities, which rely on searching for names or words in a long list of e-mails rather than requiring users to organize everything into categories to make them easier to find.

The difficulty with releasing a product in "beta" form, before it's finished, is that a product is never really finished. Most software developers just get as far as they can under the deadline they're given, then extend the deadline before releasing the product to the public, in order to get in other features they feel certain are necessary. At Google, some products never seem to come out of beta. Gmail, for example, has been on the market for five years, and is still listed as a beta product. Google has never explained why this is the case.

It's become something of a joke in the industry. Says board member Hennessy, "Sergey is frustrated with the fact that even when a product is ninety percent there, it's still in beta. It's hard to figure out how to get it to where you want it to be." But he adds that making that decision is a problem at every innovative company. Google is just more public about it.

And overall, he's extremely impressed with the company and its products. "Google's execution, certainly since the IPO, has been as good or better than any company I've ever seen," he says. "It's driven by analysis and the approach of getting all the data in front of you, so you don't spend as much time to make a decision: Is this a big issue or a small issue? Is there a quick fix or is this a major problem? That kind of thing goes on a fair amount."

By tapping the power of technology and imagination, Larry and Sergey have started morphing Google into a new kind of company; one more diversified, perhaps less focused, certainly more ambitious. But this is also dangerous territory, techno-logical landscapes in which they have neither experience nor a head start. Sometimes they wield Google as a blunt instrument. It's not the best way to win friends. This time, Google is moving into new markets in which its competitors are aware of the potential and are determined to get it right. And they know who the enemy is.

Chapter 11

Google, the Telephone Company?

A little sincerity is a dangerous thing, and a great deal of it is absolutely fatal.

—Oscar Wilde

For a while, Chris Sacca seemed to be turning Google into a phone company. A lawyer by training, he's a former Google manager whose specialty was "special initiatives." He had been hired to handle negotiations and legal work as Google went about buying up fiber optic cables laid by telecommunications companies in the late 1990s, and lying fallow since the dot-com crash.

A few years ago, he got himself into trouble with another group at Google. Google has been creating applications for cell phones for several years, but has been having trouble getting cell carriers to allow customers to install the apps on their phones. During a lecture at Oxford, someone asked him why his wireless carrier blocked customers from using Google Groups on their cell phones. It hit a sore point for Sacca. He had grown weary of the fact that most cell carriers were so resistant to change. Mostly, they want to dictate what applications people were allowed to use, and they prefer to dictate that customers use applications that the cell carriers themselves create, even though they're invariably inferior to those created by independent software companies. It's an extra source of revenue for them, and they hate giving up any control to outsiders. Sacca sympathized with the questioner, and complained that Google had even gotten letters from telephone companies telling Google to prevent people from using Google's free apps on their phones.

The media picked up on his comment and it spread. Google was at war with the cellular providers. Very soon, the mobile group within Google, which made the applications for mobile phones, complained. The group was wary of alienating the telephone companies, because it was trying to persuade them to work with Google. "The Google Mobile business got incredibly mad at me," says Sacca. "They even wrote a letter to get me fired. We'd been bullied into not saying anything."

Sacca has since left Google, but he was not fired. He left after his stock options were vested, and decided to take a break from the nonstop treadmill of working as an entrepreneur. He still praises Google's culture. "It was an exciting entrepreneurial time," he says. "We were flying under the radar. That was really fun. We were dressed in jeans and sweatshirts and moving millions of dollars around."

Sacca took his problem with the telephone companies to Larry. Fortunately, Larry had other ideas about the uproar. Recalls Sacca: "Larry's attitude was, 'Look, what we're saying here is entirely true. The wireless carriers are trying to get between us and our users. If we try to appease them, we'll lose our identity in the process. Or we can stand up and try to evolve this space into what it should be.' "

Larry's response about changing the cellular industry, in fact, was to become even more aggressive. He encouraged Sacca to pursue a bid for a wireless spectrum that the U.S. government was offering to sell to phone companies. "Larry gave me a push, to figure out how to be more of a catalyst, to help shape the wireless space."

Google the Catalyst

The role of industry catalyst has become a huge one for Larry. It explains some of the company's most confusing moves. It also causes a lot of animosity among the companies being catalyzed.

Telecommunications is Larry and Sergey's current favorite because in this area they see a picture out of whack, like a framed photograph cracked and misaligned after an earthquake. The Internet is the earthquake, and Google is the fixer trying to bring the two halves back together. On one side is the public, ready to embrace the cheaper and more robust capabilities of the Internet, the philosophy of open standards rather than closed systems controlled by large corporations, the luxury of freedom of choice. On the other are the telephone and cable companies, unwilling to reach across the chasm and embrace the changes the Internet offers—including cheaper or free services.

With that philosophy, Sacca, who is known as a ruthless negotiator, got top management to approve a bid of up to $5 billion to buy the rights to the 700 MHz wireless spectrum.

In pursuit of that goal, the bid came with a caveat. Google would bid only if the FCC stipulated that carriers keep the system "open," including a requirement that the winning bidder of one coveted section of the spectrum—known as the C-block—allow all cell phones, not just its own, to operate in the spectrum. That ensured that if another company won the bid, Google cell phones and mobile applications would still work in the spectrum.

With that move, Google started a telco war. Verizon Wireless, which has been the biggest holdout in allowing Google applications on its phones, filed a lawsuit against the FCC to try to eliminate the open-access rules. Google argued against it, and one cellular carrier, Frontline Wireless—whose board includes former FCC chairman Reed Hundt and former assistant secretary of commerce for telecommunications policy Janice Obuchowski—even asked the FCC to ban Verizon Wireless from the auction.

In the end, the FCC decided to adopt some of the terms Google was pushing for. As long as the winning bid for the C-block was at least $4.6 billion, those cell phones would also be allowed to let customers download applications created by outsiders—including Google. "When your mission is sincere, it's easy for employees and users to get behind it," says Sacca, who ran the Alternative Access Group. "We ask what we can do to increase access."

Google did bid in the spectrum auction, but did not win. (Verizon Wireless got the C-block, with a bid of $9.4 billion, while AT&T walked off with another section of the spectrum, for $6.6 billion.) But Google had achieved its goal. It took on the phone companies and won concessions that forced Verizon Wireless to allow Google's Android-based cell phones and applications—and those of others—to use the spectrum.

Even without winning the bid, Google managed to change the mobile phone industry. Says Google executive David Girouard, "It's all about the choice available to consumers." Some critics have speculated that Larry was never really serious about the bid, since Google got what it wanted without spending a penny. Sacca insists that this is not true. "Even a company as exciting and creative and maverick as Google can't throw five billion dollars around willy-nilly," says Sacca. "This was not a game or a bluff."

Google looks like a competitor to telecommunications companies. It owns thousands of miles of fiber optic cable, has dabbled in setting up free Internet access, has created an array of programs for cell phones, and has designed a free cell phone operating system called Android. The first phone based on that system, the Google G1 phone, was announced in 2008 from handset manufacturer HTC, running on T-Mobile's cellular service.

This game can be costly to Google. In 2007, its executives were in negotiations with Verizon Wireless to get the cellular company to adopt Google's mobile search application on its cell phones. But Verizon Wireless executives are not keen to take on a thorn in their sides as a partner. In early January 2008, Verizon Wireless signed a five-year deal with Microsoft, a distant third-place runner in the search engine race, to provide its mobile search and advertising services. Verizon also reportedly passed on the opportunity to be the first carrier to use the G1 phone.

Smartphone maker Nokia has reached deals with both Microsoft and Yahoo to provide search services, but not with Google. So far, Taiwan-based HTC, Sony Ericsson, Motorola, LG, ASUS, Samsung, and Toshiba are releasing phones based on the Android system, but only T-Mobile has agreed to use the phones on its service. Most telecommunications companies are reluctant to deal with Google.

Says Google CEO Schmidt, "We are critically dependent on the telco people. We also don't like closed networks, but a significant amount of their money is made that way. Android is a reminder of the potential competition, but is also an example of the way to do it right. It's a complex relationship which we're okay at but do not excel at."

One bright spot is Google's relationship with Apple. At the company's annual meeting a couple of years ago, Larry emphasized, "We love Apple. Expect us to work with them in the future." Schmidt is also on Apple's board. Steve Jobs persuaded AT&T to allow applications by third parties to run on the iPhone, and Google's apps are available on that phone.

This business is critical to Google's future. In many ways, smartphones are the new PCs. They are steadily and inevitably becoming the world's Internet devices. Google executives have said that searching and advertising are destined to become even bigger businesses on smartphones than on computers.

Getting People Online

Google executives insist the company is not really trying to become a phone company. "Owning fiber doesn't make you a telephone service provider," says Sacca. "We're pushing a lot of data between data centers, sometimes across oceans. It brings down latency."

But given Google's technological prowess, it could do so. The company's increasing moves into the telecommunications business are focused primarily on another need. Telcos (and PC makers, book publishers, Hollywood, and other industries critical to Google's success) are simply not moving fast enough for Google. Larry and Sergey want to hurry them along.

This is not pure altruism, of course. One big problem blocking Google's future is the ability to get people online. Google benefits from any move that gets more people online with faster communications, since the company currently makes all its money online. But Larry and Sergey are also trying to force the world to change, to conform to their vision of what the Internet should be: opening up the wireless spectrum, lowering the cost of cellular access, breaking down barriers that block the adoption of free ad-supported applications, and speeding up Internet communications. Google the catalyst is dragging the telecommunications industry into the Internet Age.

In the United States, this means goosing the Internet service providers, or ISPs—the telcos, cable companies, satellite networks, and others that connect people to the Internet. That is a much-needed role. The United States ranks nineteenth in the world in Internet access per capita, and U.S. "high-speed" Internet access is embarrassingly slow compared with that in such countries as Japan, Korea, and several European nations that have built out their telecommunications infrastructure to accommodate the potential of the Internet.

One can only wish that Google would become an ISP. Unlike most technology businesses, prices for Internet access have not dropped. The telcos and cable companies have little competition, because they own regional monopolies. In one of the biggest technology debates facing Congress today, Google and other Internet companies are fighting the ISPs over the subject of "net neutrality."

As it stands today, once a consumer pays for Internet access, the amount of data he ships back and forth between his computer and the Internet cloud is unlimited. Start-ups rely on this fact to create new online businesses. But ISPs, led by the telcos, argue that in order to handle the increased traffic, they need to upgrade their networks, as other countries have done. And in order to do that, they say they need more revenue, or they can't afford to spend the billions of dollars necessary to make the upgrades.

In other countries, governments have covered the costs as an expense that improves competitiveness. The telcos want Google, Yahoo, and other large online businesses to pay for it.

Cable companies have already gotten into trouble with federal regulators for slowing down Internet service to customers who download a lot of data. The ISPs now want to make it legal to charge online companies that send around a lot of data, acting as toll roads for big data hogs. This would end the neutrality of Internet access. Google argues that a company such as YouTube could never have gotten started if it had to pay telcos for transmitting its data at a time when it had no revenue. Most of Silicon Valley backs Google's view.

Sergey himself has traveled to the nation's capital to argue the point before regulators, largely unsuccessfully. In one hastily organized trip in the summer of 2006, dressed in blue jeans, a black T-shirt, and silver mesh sneakers, he failed to get meetings with key senators, including then–Senate Commerce Committee chairman Ted Stevens (R-Alaska), whose committee has huge influence on telecom legislation. The trip "wasn't very well organized," Sergey sheepishly told the *Washington Post*. "I apologize. It was a last-minute trip."[1]

On the other hand, the telcos have strong lobbies. On Sergey's trip to D.C. in 2006, he was surprised to learn that a lobbying group backed in part by AT&T had run newspaper and television ads warning that Google might "blow up" legislation designed to increase choice on cable television. "I am probably naïve," he said. "I was very surprised to see this."[2]

Google is trying to become a better Washington lobbyist. It hired people away from MCI and other telecommunications companies to help with its arguments. It's also trying to come up with alternative ways to increase telco revenue, such as location-based advertising programs when people use WiFi connections. Says Sacca: "If there are players who don't play nice with us, we ask, 'Can we incent them to do the right thing?' We want to grow opportunities for carriers to monetize their services."

Google is also investing in other companies that may provide more competition in the Internet access business. It has invested in wireless access companies, satellite companies that may be able to provide Internet access and even a company called Current Communications, which is trying to build broadband Internet connections that operate over existing electric wires in homes. "Google needs to deeply understand wireless, broadband over power lines, satellite—anything to eliminate the barriers to cheap access," says Sacca.

But Google is still a lousy lobbyist, and does a poor job of winning allies.

Free WiFi, Anyone?

Sacca came up with another idea to help people get online. What if cities themselves were to start offering free wireless access, or WiFi? After all, it would be a great incentive to offer companies considering opening offices in a city, ensuring that workers could get online even when out of the office. Sacca decided to see if he could kick-start the idea. "It started with just me. Like most things at Google, you just start it and don't ask for permission."

Sacca saw the resistance from ISPs as a dangerous trend. "There was a lot of saber rattling from the ISPs. We had a layer between us and our users. It scared me and concerned me. We spent time thinking about how do we respond to this? Policy? Sure, but we were still young in D.C."

Since San Francisco mayor Gavin Newsom is good friends with Larry and Sergey and a big fan of Google, he seemed like a good place to start. Sacca talked with the mayor in the summer of 2006 and got his approval. Google offered to install the WiFi transceivers and operate the system for free, although it would cost Google $8 million to $10 million to install it. Who could turn it down?

San Francisco could, as it turns out. Google announced that it was planning to start the system, and immediately other telecommunications companies complained. Why couldn't they bid to install the system? Perhaps they could offer a better deal, such as a service that did not include any advertising. So the San Francisco board of supervisors decided to put it up for a bid. Several telcos put together partnerships to offer the service, and Google teamed up with Earthlink. A city employee was assigned the task of reviewing the bids.

The results of the bidding were not surprising. The Google/ Earthlink bid was zero dollars, and the board of supervisors announced that the team had won. But even a free system was not good enough for some supervisors. Two of them, Chris Daly and Jake McGoldrick, began asking why Google was being given free access to San Francisco citizens, who would have to look at ads when using the service. Besides, Google would have to install the transceivers on city-owned light poles. Shouldn't it pay rent for the privilege? They began to make more demands. Google came back and sweetened the offer: it would pay the city $1 million over the first few years of the contract.

Supervisor McGoldrick complained that this was not enough. After all, Google had a profit of hundreds of millions of dollars a year. It could afford to pay more. Other groups also weighed in. Telcos and consumer advocates complained that the service would cause interference with other WiFi services. Others worried that it would produce harmful radiation. Sacca pointed out that the radiation produced was one thirteen-thousandth the level of that of a typical cell phone. He offered to get community organizations involved with free services, and to hire San Francisco workers to install the system. Some telcos sued to stop its implementation.

"We thought, we have a lot of smart wireless engineers here, what if we built one of these wireless networks to see if it works?" says Sacca. "Incumbents were saying it would never work, entrepreneurs were claiming it could do everything. I thought we could buy the equipment, hang it up, and see if it works."

Finally, Sacca decided to meet with Supervisor Chris Daly to argue for the system. There are poor neighborhoods in San Francisco where people have no Internet access, some of them in Supervisor Daly's constituency. This would be big political capital for him, Sacca argued. Google would be sure to give him credit for making the system happen. But there was another sticking point: political rivalry. Daly is one of the supervisors constantly at war with Mayor Newsom.

Sacca says Daly flatly refused to back the initiative and ended the meeting by saying, "Now this is where you just get the hell out of my office." Adds Sacca, "It was fascinating and disheartening. I was so upset, I just fumed in the lobby. I didn't want to leave the building."

San Francisco still does not have a citywide WiFi system, although Mayor Newsom has managed to install smaller WiFi networks at city housing projects under a grant from AT&T.

In the meantime, while this controversy was raging in San Francisco, Google got a similar proposal to fly through the government regulators in its own town, Mountain View. That system has now been up and running for over a year, and Google says the interference concerns have not panned out. "The experience in Mountain View was really fulfilling," says Sacca. "We did community meetings entirely in Spanish" to promote the idea. "The usage was concentrated most heavily in the poorest parts of the town, including some Hispanic neighborhoods. For some of these people, it was their lifeline."

Google still wants to see more WiFi across the world. It funded and helped launch a company called Meraki Networks, which makes wireless transceivers that people can buy not only to create a wireless connection for themselves, but also to offer their WiFi connections to others. Some do it for free, but others can charge for the access, using an online billing system provided and run by Meraki. The system is gaining popularity in San Francisco.

But Google never saw this as a new business opportunity. It was mainly interested in the catalyst role—getting local municipalities to start thinking about the possibilities. "The goal wasn't to build WiFi in every town," says Sacca. "Just one or two. Hopefully, cut them some air, act as a catalyst." And this did happen. Many cities started installing municipal WiFi systems, including Philadelphia, New Orleans, Houston, Chicago, Atlanta, Portland, and Boston. In many of these cities, existing ISPs sued to keep it from happening. After Verizon Communications and other ISPs lobbied the Pennsylvania state legislature, it passed a law forbidding any city in that state to build any WiFi network without giving the private sector first crack at it.

The idea of free WiFi as proposed by Google is now effectively dead. It's been hard for companies to create an effective advertising model that would support free WiFi. If anybody could have done so, it would have been Google, but the company says it's through with experimenting with the concept. Earthlink, one of the companies trying to make a business out of municipal WiFi, is facing financial troubles and has decided to get out of the municipal WiFi business. As a result, Philadelphia is shutting down its Earthlink-based WiFi system, and others are following that lead.

Perhaps it was a bad idea to begin with. The old WiFi technology that's been used so far was inadequate, since the signals cannot pass through walls or other obstructions in cities. Craig Settles, a municipal WiFi consultant at Successful.com, believes

Google did a disservice to the concept by leading cities to believe they could get WiFi for free. In retrospect, Sacca believes he offered too much up front. He should have first offered to install the system for a few million dollars, then negotiated down. Mayor Gavin Newsom believes that everything fell apart because the city didn't simply jump on Google's offer immediately and instead let too many other companies get involved. "If we had just worked with Google, it would have happened," he says.

Google is getting better at the political game, and it still has a chance to make change happen. There are new alternatives on the rise. One is the "white space" between broadcast TV channel frequencies—buffer zones created to keep one channel's signal from interfering with the one next to it. As broadcast TV goes digital, the FCC has decided to open up the frequencies for other uses, including WiFi. These signals can pass through walls. It was controversial, with broadcasters and entertainers lobbying against it, saying there would still be interference, and Google and others lobbying for it. This was one of Larry's pet projects. After testing, the FCC has decided that interference won't be a problem, and it approved its use. Larry couldn't help getting in a dig at his opponents in a posting on the company's blog: "As an engineer, I was also really gratified to see that the FCC decided to put science over politics," he wrote. "For years the broadcasting lobby and others have tried to spread fear and confusion about this technology, rather than allow the FCC's engineers to simply do their work."

Another is a proposal by the FCC to auction off a 25-MHz

swath of spectrum in the 2,155-MHz band, with the requirement that the winning bidder use some of it to offer free WiFi across the country. Even Settles believes this proposal could work.

Google has not given any indication of how it might participate in these new proposals. But given its vested interest in getting more people online cheaply and without restrictions, it's highly likely that it will participate in some way. The moves and lobbying Google has already done "will ultimately lead to more Internet access," says Sacca. And, as he notes, "Google has staggeringly high resources to be applied to the world's biggest problems."

Google may yet look more like a telecommunications company in the future. And, once again, people will scratch their heads and wonder why Larry and Sergey wanted to get involved in something so far removed from the search business.

Chapter 12

Thinking Beyond Search

The World's Problems, Real and Fanciful

The sad truth is that excellence makes people nervous.

—Shana Alexander, journalist and author

L arry and Sergey took three years to find someone they trusted to guide their philanthropic organization, Google .org. The wait was worth it. Once again, it's hard to imagine that they could have found a better person for the job.

Dr. Larry Brilliant is the quintessential Baby Boomer. Born in 1944, he has an M.D. and is a specialist in preventive medicine and public health. He attended Woodstock, the Burning Man festival of its day, and studied under a yogi in India, who encouraged him to start a mission to banish smallpox in that country—which he did, working with the World Health Organization. For a while, back in Northern California, he was Jerry Garcia's personal physician.

Brilliant says he struggles with the typical Baby Boomer's restless ambition, but at least he puts it to good use. He's founder and director of the Seva Foundation, which works to eliminate preventable and curable blindness in countries around the world. He has worked with the Centers for Disease Control on a smallpox bioterrorism response effort. Following up on his role presiding over the last natural case of smallpox in the world, he later worked on a campaign to eliminate polio in developing countries. Most recently, he volunteered in Sri Lanka for tsunami relief. In February 2006 he received a $100,000 TED Prize (part of the Technology, Entertainment, Design conference) for his wish to build a global early warning system that can detect new pandemics or disasters before they get out of control.

Brilliant also has an eclectic background as an executive and board member. He was cofounder of The Well, the first online virtual community in the 1970s. He was also CEO of the broadband company SoftNet Systems Inc. and holds a telecommunications technology patent. Today he serves as a member of the strategic advisory committee for the venture capital firm KPCB, and sits on the boards of the Skoll Foundation, Health Metrics Network, Omidyar Network, Humanity United, and InSTEDD, an organization applying technological tools to improve disaster response.

He says he first heard about Google's philanthropic arm, then called the Google Foundation, when he was laid up in a refugee camp in Sri Lanka with typhoid fever. "I was mildly delirious, and in order to stay conscious I forced myself to translate every Hindi newspaper I could get, because it was hard, and otherwise

I would pass out with typhoid." In one article, he read about the Google Foundation. It included an e-mail address that people interested in a job with the organization could write to. So he sent the e-mail and asked to learn more about the foundation. He never got a response. But, he says, he may have gotten the e-mail address wrong. "The article was all in Hindi, so I'm not even sure if my e-mail got through."

But when he returned to the United States, Larry and Sergey found him. It started at TED (Technology, Entertainment, Design), an organization run by the private, nonprofit Sapling Foundation. Its annual conference attracts luminaries on a par with the World Economic Forum. In March 2006, some TED members encouraged Brilliant to give some talks and meet with people at companies that were part of TED, in order to get some support for his wish. He gave a talk in Woodside, a tony Silicon Valley town populated by venture capitalists and wealthy executives, about his TED wish and his work eradicating smallpox. Unbeknownst to him, Larry Page and Eric Schmidt were in the back of the room. One of them turned to the other and said, "Let's hire him." Brilliant is not sure which one.

He then ran into a Google executive who told him, "We were just talking about you as a candidate to run Google.org. We've been looking for somebody for several years, we've interviewed thousands of people, and we can't find the right person." Brilliant says he wasn't interested at first. He hadn't reported to a boss for about forty years, and didn't want to. But at a dinner at Google board member John Doerr's house, Doerr emphasized that it was an extraordinary opportunity. Brilliant says Doerr told him, "You've got to go meet with Larry and Sergey. Just go in, close the door, spend the day with them, and see if you don't think they're the most wonderful people in the world." He did, and they were. Brilliant has become one of the pair's biggest fans. In February 2006 he became executive director of Google.org. (In early 2009, he turned over control of Google.org to another executive and became Google's "chief philanthropy evangelist," more of a lobbyist, organizer, and promoter of Google's philanthropic ideas.)

Changing the World

Google.org is endowed with three million shares of Google stock, worth over $1 billion. That pales in comparison to one of the biggest private philanthropies, the Bill and Melinda Gates Foundation, of which Bill Gates himself is now co-chair. That foundation was created in 1994 with an endowment of $94 million. But Gates, who just recently started focusing most of his efforts there, has expanded it to over $35 billion. It does extraordinary work in health and education issues, much of it in the developing world. Gates's mother was a prominent philanthropist with United Way, and he had set an agenda for himself when he was very young: make a fortune as an entrepreneur first, then become a philanthropist. He was true to his word.

The difference with Larry and Sergey, says Brilliant, is that they're dedicated to making Google the core of philanthropic work at such a young age. "When you're older and you've lost somebody, when you've been touched with mortality, had a birth or a near death, seen the futility of material things, you will wax philosophic about the meaning of life and duty and making the morally right decisions," says Brilliant. "But in young people, my experience has been that that's rare. That's what was so impressive about Larry and Sergey. I was double their age and they had thought more deeply about some of the moral issues of technology and business than I had."

Brilliant has had a strong influence on the organization. Larry and Sergey were deeply interested in his background dealing with disease. After three weeks on the job, Larry came to his office and said they should think about health. They spent a year going through thousands of different proposals that had been submitted to them, from dealing with water crises to the disparity between rich and poor, to women's genital mutilation in certain countries, to HIV/AIDS.

Notably, Brilliant made his TED wish part of Google.org. One of its initiatives is development of a program to use the power of information technology to create a proactive system that can predict and help prevent infectious diseases, rather than just reacting to them once they've spread. The organization studies factors that spread disease, such as climate change, deforestation, rising international travel, and human contact with animals. It focuses on developing countries, and tracks diseases and natural disasters.

Another initiative of which Brilliant is extremely proud

is called "Inform and Empower." Again focused on developing countries, it has as its mission to inform the populations of developing countries of services available to them from their own governments. Too frequently people don't even know what programs they might be able to tap, and the program is designed to empower them to demand those services, ranging from education to improving water quality to finding a doctor. Sometimes the governments themselves are not aware that the services they're paying for are not actually being provided. That program also funds nonprofit NGOs (nongovernmental organizations) to act as scorekeepers to track who's getting schools or physicians in their area.

Brilliant says this program can even empower the governments to provide new services. "Some countries are post-Soviet, and many countries in Africa are post-conflict, and these are not necessarily governments that have a long tradition of delivering complex services to huge numbers of people. So we can help, with tools, with computer systems, and then we can help empower communities to know which of these things are important. That's a really great initiative with Google's core principles," he says.

But Larry and Sergey are still the go-to people for approval. They like to analyze the programs and look for practical ways to implement them and measure progress. When Brilliant presented the proposal for the Inform and Empower program to Larry and Sergey, he came armed with several objectives: to improve the ability of governments to render service, to improve the ability of people to find out about those services, and to get a scorekeeper.

Larry and Sergey discussed this, and pointed out that the important issue isn't whether the government or an NGO is keeping score; the important thing is the result. So they said each program should also set a goal—that 80 percent of the people affected should know the quality of the water they drink, the quality of education their kids get, and the quality of the health care they receive. "Their thinking went immediately above the tactics to the results," says Brilliant. "That's the way they think. They go to the highest level and they externalize it."

Brilliant, who is better read than most journalists interviewing him, compares Larry and Sergey's thinking to that of Immanuel Kant when he wrote philosophical arguments about what actions constituted the greatest good in the world. Kant described the "categorical imperative," which suggests choosing the good work you do by asking yourself, "What if everybody got this good thing?" Says Brilliant, "The idea is to look to the universality of the good. That's the way Larry and Sergey think. Their minds are in a different paradigm."

Another favorite obsession Larry and Sergey share is dealing with climate change. They had started initiatives to explore those problems before Brilliant arrived. Larry is the one who is particularly interested in this issue. In 2007 he gave a talk at the annual meeting of the American Association for the Advancement of Science (AAAS) in which he argued that the scientists should make it a point to look for solutions to global warming and to make sure the public knows about them.

He then decided to show them how to do it. This led to two

initiatives: developing utility scale renewable energy that's cheaper than coal-based power plants, dubbed RE<C; and speeding the development of technology for plug-in hybrid cars, called RechargeIT.

These programs provide grants to, and make investments in, organizations working on these goals. But Google takes it further than that. Some of the things the company spends money on make no sense for a software company. For one, Google has its own renewable energy R&D group, complete with engineers and energy experts to work on technologies such as solar thermal power, wind power, and geothermal energy. Within a few years, Larry wants to build a one-gigawatt plant, enough to power a city the size of San Francisco.

Notably, the types of research Google is focusing on are the ones most likely to produce quick results. Solar thermal power, for example—one of the items Larry touted at the AAAS meeting—consists of using mirrors to focus the sun on vats of water or oil, generating steam to run electrical turbines. Solar electric cells are still too inefficient to convert the sun's energy directly into electricity on a large scale.

To say the least, it's an unusual task for a software company to tackle. But that's Larry for you. In a blog posting, he explained the reasons he felt it was something Google should take on: "Our new initiative isn't just about Google's energy needs; we're seeking to accelerate the pace at which clean energy technologies are developing, so they can rival the economics of coal quickly. We've gained expertise in designing and building large-scale, energy-intensive facilities by building data centers that lead the industry in efficiency. We want to apply the same creativity and innovation to the challenge of generating inexpensive renewable electricity at scale. By combining talented technologists, great partners and large investments, we have an opportunity to quickly push this technology forward."

The philosophy is "hybrid philanthropy," with Google both funding others and trying to develop the technology itself. "It's not a tangent," insists Brilliant. "The independent charge to Google.org is to try to address some of the greatest problems by using the fortune Google has, and this is one of the gravest crises. How could we do less? If all we did was give money, we would be falling short of hybrid philanthropy. For the people who say it doesn't make sense, I would point out that we do lots of hardware stuff at Google. This company, because of its success, touches on every controversial aspect of life. The darkest and brightest of our species flow through Google."

And this collaboration between Google.org and Google.com is only going to increase. A big part of the reason Brilliant turned over daily management of Google.org to Megan Smith, Google's vice president of New Business Development, was to better link Google technologists to Google.org programs. In a blog posting announcing the change, Brilliant wrote, "[O]ur greatest impact has come when we've attacked problems in ways that make the most of Google's strengths in technology and information." Smith will provide that bridge.

This is the serious, altruistic side to Larry and Sergey and their desire to do great things for the world. They also have a more whimsical side, and a side that thinks there's almost no end to what they can do with their unexpected, extraordinary wealth.

Space Age Ideas

Larry and Sergey like to think big. They pursue their own interests no matter how remote they are from Google—or even this planet. Some are as flighty as space travel; others are as grounded as the DNA that makes them who they are.

Larry and Sergey have a keen interest in space travel. They have even reached an agreement to build a new corporate campus on NASA's Ames Research Center nearby in Mountain View, with a promise to cooperate with the organization on research projects. There's no word yet on what those projects may be, but Google has already started working with NASA on some fun mapping projects—providing space enthusiasts with images that simulate virtual flyovers of the moon and Mars—just as Google Maps can do virtual flyovers of your local neighborhood.

In 2008, Sergey made a $5 million investment in a Virginia company called Space Adventures, which plans to buy flights on Russian Soyuz rockets to the International Space Station and sell them to wealthy tourists. Expect Sergey to be on the first tourist flight, scheduled in 2011. He's no doubt driving his life insurance company apoplectic.

In 2007, Google announced the Google Lunar X Prize, in which Google will award up to $30 million for any projects that successfully land an unmanned rover on the moon and send back a gigabyte of images to earth. Larry and Sergey have also bandied about an idea for a "space elevator," a serious proposal that some scientists have promoted, in which a cable is tethered from the ground to a counterweight in geosynchronous orbit in space. The idea is that, rather than using rockets to launch payloads into space, the satellites or other items can simply be run up the cable. Part of Schmidt's job is to keep some of these more fanciful ideas from getting too much publicity.

And then there's the planned trip to Mars, called Project Virgle. This one was announced on April 1, 2008. It's described on Google's Web site: "Earth has issues, and it's time humanity got started on a Plan B. So, starting in 2014, Virgin founder Richard Branson and Google co-founders Larry Page and Sergey Brin will be leading hundreds of users on one of the grandest adventures in human history: Project Virgle, the first permanent human colony on Mars."

Google has a "one-hundred-year plan" for this project and offered to let people participate by submitting thirty-second YouTube videos explaining why they want to live on Mars. Says Sergey, "If you're chosen you're going to get to join Larry, Richard and myself on the planet Mars sometime in the next 20 years.[1]"

For Love and Money

On a more serious side, Larry and Sergey have both invested in Silicon Valley's Tesla Motors, feeding their desire to see cars hit the market without polluting the air (and perhaps their desire to drive a really snazzy zero-emissions sports car). Tesla is building electric-powered convertibles that look like a cross between a Porsche Boxster and a Maserati. The first vehicles, which every wealthy Silicon Valley executive drools over (zero to sixty in four seconds), cost over $100,000. Both Larry and Sergey bought at least one. Later versions will go for $50,000 to $65,000.

Sergey has also combined his love life and interest in science with another Google investment. In May 2007, Google made a $3.9 million investment in 23andMe, a biotech company co-founded by his wife, Anne Wojcicki. Regulatory filings on that investment were the first confirmation that the pair was actually married. 23andMe creates a system that allows individuals to learn about their own genetic makeup, make sense of their genetic information, accelerate research into customized drug delivery systems, and help personalize the field of medicine. One more piece of metadata to add to the list.

It's just more of the founders' love of exploring radical ideas. The culture at Google encourages far-out thinking, on the philosophy that one never knows what might turn out to be something really interesting that the founders actually want to pursue.

Google brainstorming includes the purely fanciful. A couple of years ago, venture capitalist Steve Jurvetson, on a visit to Google, took a picture of a whiteboard labeled "GOOGLE'S MASTER PLAN," and posted it on his blog. It appears to be a real outline of Google's interests—some of them have come to pass or are well within the realm of possibility, including searches for TV, games, reviews, ski conditions, sports, traffic reports, music, comics, and gossip—but other Googlers had added their own graffiti to the whiteboard to suggest other ideas, apparently as another April Fool's Day joke. Some samples: "Hire rogue scientists" with a link to "Hire Richard Branson." Other trajectories included "Space Station," "Space travel," "Teleportation," "Orbital mind control," and "Weather control." And two of the entries that appear with the grouping of genuine items are a "Google operating system" (presumably for PCs) and an entry simply labeled "Casino."

Certainly, some unusual ideas have already become Google products. Take Mail Goggles, for example, an idea dreamed up by Google engineer Jon Perlow and introduced within Google Labs in October 2008. The press has labeled it Gmail's "drunk e-mail protector." When enabled, it checks to see if you're really sober enough to send that e-mail to your girlfriend, your boss, or anyone else late on a Friday night, requiring you to solve some simple math problems before it will send your e-mail. It's active only on late weekend nights.

Some ideas are more practical. Google is working on software that will analyze energy use from "smart meters" in homes, in order to provide people with suggestions on how to cut their energy bills (and to provide another product that dovetails with Google.org). Other projects are merely fanciful. In February 2002, Google added Klingon to the list of languages used for search results.

And rumors of new Google products are rampant. Aside from the Google PC, Google is said to be working on a communications router to compete with Cisco Systems, which will help speed up Internet communications. In February 2008, the stock of struggling CNET Networks, which provides tech news and product reviews, rose 7 percent on rumors that Google was thinking of investing in the company. (So far, it hasn't happened.) There have even been rumors that Google was interested in buying Sprint and *really* getting into the cell phone business.

Everyone likes to speculate, but there's no telling where Larry and Sergey will take their company next. There's one thing that's certain: they are going to be breaking rules, pissing people off, and trying to make the world a better place for decades to come. Love them or despise them, everyone must contend with them. They are having greater impacts on the business world and on people's lifestyles than any other business executives in the world. Their hearts are in the right place, even if their heads are sometimes not.

But then, Larry and Sergey have always been difficult to figure out. Venture capitalist Mike Speiser will attest to that. In early 2000, when Speiser was still an entrepreneur at online ratings site Epinions, he met Larry at a social gathering for entrepreneurs called Round Zero. The conversation turned to politics, and he was taken aback by Larry's attitude. "I'm all for questioning the current orthodoxy," says Speiser. "But Larry effortlessly ignored all of the laws and customs of the day. I remember thinking that Silicon Valley is loaded with self-proclaimed Libertarians, but this guy is an anarchist."

Larry was so unusual, in fact, that he made Speiser uncomfortable. At the time, Speiser had difficulty seeing Google succeeding with Larry as one of the company's top leaders. But he has since come to appreciate that much of Google's success is likely a result of Larry's lack of respect for authority. "My parents taught me that many of the great scientists throughout time succeeded because they ignored conventional wisdom and followed their own instincts. I now realize that entrepreneurship is no different. The people who break the current orthodoxy make others uncomfortable. And they are also the ones who change the world."

With Google and their sudden wealth at their disposal, Larry and Sergey now have enormous power to make those changes, and they will continue to do so for decades to come. They're like Harry Potter after he discovered he was a wizard and got his wand. You can expect great things from them.

Afterword to the Paperback Edition

Google: The New Microsoft

Larry and Sergey's magic wands just got more powerful. In January 2011, the company announced that CEO Eric Schmidt was handing the reins back to the cofounders. Larry Page is now the CEO, and will focus on product development and technology strategy. Sergey Brin will devote his time to "strategic products," particularly new product development. Schmidt becomes "executive chairman," an unusual title that has led to a lot of speculation that he will eventually leave the company altogether, but will remain a strategic adviser to the pair.

Why the changes? Nobody knows for sure. But Google has been struggling to be dominant in a few new arenas, social networking in particular, an area the team sees as critical to its future. Interestingly, Sergey's new devotion to strategic products seems to suggest that he's taken the most important product development away from Larry. Perhaps it's a move to make the product development process work faster with better results.

It's hard to say if Schmidt wanted to leave or if Larry and Sergey wanted to regain control. Schmidt has nothing left to prove and walks away with a new, $100 million stock bonus. It will be granted over four years, as long as he remains with the company, indicating that Larry and Sergey want him to stay a while.

The new structure does seem likely to streamline the decision-making process, something Google needs right now. Instead of a three-person team agreeing on major decisions, Larry will focus on the basic products and running the company, while Sergey will focus on getting the company into the most important new areas. That may be the most significant change—getting new products out the door faster, with smaller teams and better coordination.

Larry and Sergey will continue to jump on the latest trends, try to pioneer new products that leverage Google's strength in the search engine sphere, spend billions of dollars on acquisitions to broaden their reach, and pour millions of dollars into Internet technology in order to catalyze faster growth of the medium.

In fact, despite what its executives may say, Google is no longer just a search company; it's an Internet software company. Larry and Sergey are on a grand quest to provide software for every device that connects to the Internet. Google is, in short, the Microsoft of the Internet generation.

Despite a popular view that Google isn't as innovative as it once was, it has already established itself in many fields of technology that are being transformed by the Internet: web browsers, e-mail, online maps, blogging software, online video, mobile phone software, photo editing software, instant messaging, and online productivity tools, to name a few. And it's just getting started.

In the PC era, the battle came down to Microsoft vs. Apple. Microsoft's Windows was never quite as good as Apple's Macs (once Steve Jobs returned to Apple). Jobs's strategy was to control everything from hardware to software design himself. That made his products more expensive and limited Apple to the top end of the market—the Mercedes of computing. Microsoft's Bill Gates licensed his software to all PC makers, giving him a much larger mass-market share. A similar scenario is now taking shape in the market for Internet devices, but with Google in Microsoft's old role.

Google's Android phone operating system is taking off as Internet connections for smart phones become the hottest trend in electronics. In August 2010, a study by the Nielsen Company showed that Android phone sales have started outpacing every other smart phone operating system. The Blackberry by Research in Motion (RIM) and Apple's iPhone still hold the number one and two spots respectively, but the Android is catching up. In the second quarter of 2010, according to Nielsen, Android took 27 percent of smart phone sales, up from 6 percent at the end of 2009, while the iPhone took 23 percent, down from 34 percent. BlackBerry got 33 percent of the market, down from 39 percent. Microsoft's share dropped to 11 percent from 13 percent. The Android clearly has the momentum to take over the competition.

That could change, of course, as Apple and RIM release new designs, but the only phones with cachet are the iPhone and Android. Also, as the iPhone finally migrates to the Verizon network, releasing it from the limitation of only being available to AT&T customers, it could gain new momentum. But Jobs is sticking to his strategy of creating the entire phone himself, which means there is only one manufacturer, while Google is licensing its system to all of the phone makers except Apple.

A recent survey by a mobile-software tools provider called Appcelerator found that while the iPhone is the leader in downloadable applications right now, a majority of mobile phone "apps" developers see a bigger future in Google's Android mobile phone operating system. Why? The Android system is available on more than sixty devices and several mobile networks, and the applications do not have to be cleared by the man at the top.

Even Apple's customers are starting to feel that Google is taking the lead in smart phone features. A research firm called Vision Critical surveyed iPhone users to find out what they think their phones lack, and the list of features they came up with—the ability to run on a choice of wireless carriers, the ability to run on a 4G network, an 8 megapixel camera, a larger display, a removable battery, and a physical keyboard—reads like a list of the technology already available on the newest Android phones.

The other hot new trend is the iPad from Apple as standard netbooks, essentially small laptop computers, are a cooling trend. Once again, Steve Jobs has worked his magic to create a new category of computer. That could be trouble for Google and its

Chrome operating system, which is targeted at netbooks. Further, an iPad competitor from RIM was scheduled to arrive in the first quarter of 2011, a prospect that drove up the company's stock by 40 percent from August to December 2010, despite the fact that nobody was sure how well the new device would sell. Google is likely to revamp its own netbook design in order to directly compete with these new tablet computers, probably under Sergey's leadership. The release of the first Chrome OS devices was delayed by six months to mid-2011, so it will have to play catch-up to Apple. However, that's a page directly out of Microsoft's old playbook: keep redesigning until the product is competitive. Microsoft, of course, is also trying to enter this category.

Google is also taking on Amazon's Kindle e-book reader. After Google's troubles with publishers over digitizing out-of-print books, it has adopted the strategy of helping publishers and brick-and-mortar bookstores compete with Amazon. Jeff Bezos is a hard negotiator and has been pressuring publishers to sell him books at cut-rate prices in order to pass on savings to customers. Google and Apple are both selling e-books on their own, on terms more favorable to publishers, which has decreased the pressure on publishers to accede to Amazon's demands. Google is also offering independent bookstores the opportunity to sell its e-books on their own Web sites, which could take more market share from Amazon if the independent sellers attract loyal customers to their sites. Of course, it's still very uncertain how all this will play out.

There's one important market in which Google is struggling. Larry and Sergey are intensely interested in cracking the social networking market, but have not yet been able to come close to Facebook's prominent position. In November 2010, Google changed its Terms of Service so that other companies could not access Google's contact list—which lets users import their Gmail contacts—unless the other company reciprocates. Facebook has so far refused to let its users export their contact lists to Google, although it does have deals allowing both Yahoo and Microsoft's Hotmail to access Facebook contacts. Both Facebook and Google are trying to integrate social networking with e-mail, instant messaging, games, and other online products, but Google is struggling to come up with a smooth system that pleases its customers. Its projects in this area have been variously called Google Me, +1, and Google Games, and reports say the company is having trouble bringing it all together.

One possible scenario is that Google would use its considerable resources to buy Facebook. So far, that idea has been a nonstarter with Facebook founder and CEO Mark Zuckerberg. Zuckerberg is not willing to give up control of a company with so much promise for its own IPO and his personal wealth, and he's enjoying his prestige; *Time* magazine named him 2010's Person of the Year.

In the meantime, Google has been investing in other social networking companies. It bought SocialDeck, a social gaming company for mobile phones, paid some $200 million for social game maker Slide, and bought a payment platform called Jambool for $70 million to make it easier for customers to pay for social networking games. Additionally, it invested a reported $150 million to $200 million in social gaming company Zynga (the maker of Farmville). A report in businessinsider.com says Sergey championed this deal.

Aside from these big deals, Google has a $100 million venture fund to invest in smaller companies in fields as diverse as online advertising, smart grid technology, biotechnology, and green vehicles. Altogether, Google has bought at least eighty-five companies since its founding, according to a Wikipedia list.[1]

Larry and Sergey are also trying to use the company's wealth to push for better development of Internet access technology across the United States. In its role as an industry catalyst, Google announced a contest among cities in the United States with the prize being a free ultra-high speed broadband network. It will be a fiber-based network with speeds up to one gigabit per second, one hundred times the speed most people in the United States have access to. On Google's blog, the project's managers noted the real goal of the contest is "to experiment with new ways to help make Internet access better and faster for everyone."[2] Maybe this initiative will force U.S. phone and cable companies to start investing in decent Internet access for everyone.

Finally, Google TV has been making news lately. It's an Android-based set-top box technology built directly into new TV sets that will bring together Internet and television programming, computer applications, and digital video recording into one device. The device's competition, Apple TV, is now starting to gain more traction than Google's version, although it does not have as many features as Google TV. Google's product clearly needs refinement. Perhaps this will be made a priority under Sergey's leadership. One big advantage Google may have is the ability to search for programs online and on the cable networks. Comcast is trying to fend off Google TV with its own alternative, called Xcalibur, and some networks are resisting giving Google access to their programs unless it pays for them. But this is a device that could radically transform the way we use television and force the Internet into sharper competition with TV programming.

Of course, becoming such a powerhouse has placed a lot of attention on Google. Government agencies around the world are scrutinizing its moves for antitrust violations. In early July, 2010, the European Union's antitrust chief said he was looking "very carefully" at allegations that Google unfairly ranks competitors' sites lower in search results. The irony here is that one of the main reasons Google became successful in the first place is that among all the major search engines, Google was the only one to refuse to bias its search results. There is no discernible evidence that Larry and Sergey have changed their strategy now. Type any company stock ticker name into Google, for example, and Yahoo Finance appears first. Larry and Sergey have always been adamant that search results must always be unbiased. But competitors complain and regulators, wary of Google's increasing power, will listen.

Other controversies surrounding Google's tactics continue

unabated. News organizations such as Rupert Murdoch's News Corp. are still threatening Google with lawsuits for stealing snippets of news from its publications. In addition, Viacom was dealt a setback in its suit against YouTube over copyright infringement when a U.S. court ruled against Viacom in June 2010, but Viacom says it will appeal.

More and more people are also becoming skeptical of Google's "Don't Be Evil" philosophy. That philosophy is being put to its biggest test now as it struggles with the Chinese government over censorship. When hackers broke into Google customers' e-mail accounts in China in early 2010, Sergey was irate. Saying that the hack targeted Chinese dissidents, he made it clear that he thought the attack had government backing. This event pushed Sergey too far and he announced that Google was no longer willing to censor itself in China. Google moved its operations to Hong Kong, where the laws are more liberal, and stopped censoring its search results. But it has to renew its license to continue doing business in China every year. Google submitted its application on June 30, 2010, the last day it could file, and Chinese officials were slow to approve it, but did so in the end. Google will face tough scrutiny on this from China every year. It would not be surprising to see Google lose its license sometime in the near future.

However, leaving China would be an enormous blow to Google's future. Microsoft CEO Steve Ballmer has made it clear that he has no problem doing business in China and censoring his company's search results, and the Chinese search engine Baidu continues to gain market share. If Google drops out of

China completely, it will be giving up a huge and growing market. If it compromises, its reputation as a corporation fighting against evil will take a big hit. The battle of wills is going to be intense and important to Google's future. For Larry and Sergey, it is a constant fight between revenue and principle.

Nevertheless, Google's momentum will continue to grow along with the challenges it faces. Becoming the new Microsoft may not be the description Larry and Sergey would like to have, but it is inevitable. Years ago when Microsoft's then-CEO Bill Gates was asked if new developments in technology could make his company obsolete, he scoffed, asserting (with an amazing lack of insight to the rising danger of the Internet) that as long as there were computers in the world, Microsoft's opportunities would stay strong. Now Larry and Sergey could make a similar claim: As long as the Internet is a powerful force in computing, Google's prospects—and the controversies it faces—are limitless.

Notes

All first-person accounts and quotes for this book, unless otherwise identified, are from interviews conducted by the book's author, or by Kim Girard or Andrea Orr for this book. Some of the interviews were conducted as early as June 2004. Some of the interviews at Stanford were also used for an article in *Stanford* magazine, "Net Assets: How Stanford's Computer Science Department Changed the Way We Get Information," by Richard L. Brandt, referenced elsewhere in these notes.

Introduction: The World's Librarians

1. John Ince, Podcast: "Lost Google Tapes," http://www.podventure zone.com, posted January 5, 2007.
2. "Sergey Brin and Anne Wojcicki Get Married," Commongate.com, http://web2.commongate.com/post/Sergey_Brin_and_Anne_Wojcicki_Get_Married/, posted May 13, 2007.
3. Clint Boulton, "Has Chrome Pushed Google over the Evil Edge?" Google Watch, http://googlewatch.eweek.com/content/crystal_ball/has_chrome_pushed_google_over_the_evil_edge.html, posted December 13, 2008.

4. Clint Boulton, "The Evil of Google Is Steeped in Perception, Potential," Google Watch, http://googlewatch.eweek.com/content/evil_google/the_evil_of_google_is_steeped_in_perception_potential.html, posted January 5, 2009.

5. Nicholas Carlson, "The 5 Most Laughable Terms of Service on the Net," Valleywag, http://valleywag.gawker.com/5044902/the-5-most-laughable-terms-of-service#c7571247, posted September 3, 2008.

6. Matt Cutts, "Google Does Not Want Rights to Things You Do Using Chrome," Mattcutts.com, http://www.mattcutts.com/blog/google-chrome-license-agreement/, posted September 3, 2008.

7. Matt Asay, "Google: A little more like Microsoft every day," The Open Road, http://news.cnet.com/8301-13505_3-10123944-16.html?tag=mncol;txt, posted December 16, 2008.

Chapter 1: Arbiters of Cyberspace

1. Guy Rolnik, "I've been very lucky in my life," *Ha'aretz*, May 24, 2008.

2. Ibid.

3. Brenna McBride, "The Ultimate Search," *College Park* magazine, University of Maryland, Spring 2000.

4. The reporter who conducted the interview, John Ince, has posted recordings of his interviews at PodTech.Net, http://www.podtech.net/classic/search/The+Lost+Google+Tapes.

5. Speech to the Commonwealth Club of California, March 21, 2001.

Chapter 2: Accidental Entrepreneurs

1. Richard L. Brandt, "Net Assets: How Stanford's Computer Science Department Changed the Way We Get Information," *Stanford Magazine*, November/December 2004.

2. Valérie Issarny, Michel Banâtre, Boris Charpiot, and Jean-Marc Menaud, *Lecture Notes in Computer Science*, October 1999.

3. Ince, "Lost Google Tapes."
4. Ibid.
5. Ibid.
6. Ibid.
7. Ibid.
8. Ibid.
9. John Heilemann, "Journey to the (Revolutionary, Evil-Hating, Cash-Crazy, and Possibly Self-Destructive) Center of Google," *GQ*, February 2009.
10. Om Malik, "How Google Is That?" *Forbes*, October 4, 1999, http://www.forbes.com/1999/10/04/feat_print.html.
11. Catherine Elsworth, "The Man Who Googled Himself $1 Billion," Telegraph.co.uk, October 5, 2004, http://www.telegraph.co.uk/culture/3624998/The-man-who-Googled-himself-1-billion.html.
12. Ince, "Lost Google Tapes."

Chapter 3: Controlled Chaos

1. Evan Carmichael, "Lesson #1: Don't Be Evil," Evancarmichael.com, http://www.evancarmichael.com/Famous-Entrepreneurs/645/Lesson-1-Dont-Be-Evil.html.
2. Stephen Foley, "Google Founders Need Cool Heads as Their Internet Hothouse Overheats," *The Independent*, May 12, 2006.
3. Adam Lashinsky, "Can Google Three-peat?" *Fortune*, January 31, 2008.
4. Ibid.
5. Ibid.
6. Joe Nocera, "On Day Care, Google Makes a Rare Fumble," *New York Times*, July 5, 2008.

Chapter 4: Larry and Sergey's Corporate Vision

1. Karsten Lemm, "Google's First Steps," Ubergizmo.com, http://www.ubergizmo.com/15/archives/2008/09/googles_first_steps.html, posted September 7, 2008.

2. Randall Stross, *Planet Google: One Company's Audacious Plan to Organize Everything We Know*, New York: Free Press, 2008.
3. Ince, "Lost Google Tapes."
4. David Sheff, "Google Guys," *Playboy*, September 2004.
5. Heilemann, "Journey to the (Revolutionary, Evil-hating, Cash-crazy, and Possibly Self-destructive) Center of Google."
6. Ince, "Lost Google Tapes."

Chapter 5: Advertising for the Masses

1. Saul Hansell, "Yahoo to Charge for Guaranteeing a Spot on Its Index," *New York Times*, March 2, 2004.
2. Information about Yahoo's paid inclusion program is posted at http://searchmarketing.yahoo.com/srchsb/ssb.php.
3. Thomas S. Kuhn, *The Structure of Scientific Revolutions*, Chicago: University of Chicago Press, 1992.
4. Clayton M. Christensen, *The Innovator's Dilemma: When New Technologies Cause Great Firms to Fail*, Cambridge, Mass.: Harvard Business School Press, 1997.
5. Lemm, "Google's First Steps."
6. "In Search of the Real Google," *Time*, February 12, 2006.
7. Robert A. Guth, "Microsoft Bid to Beat Google Builds on a History of Misses," *Wall Street Journal*, January 16, 2009.
8. Ibid.
9. Yi-Wyn Yen, "Google Co-founder Takes Shot at Microsoft's Bid for Yahoo," Techland blog, CNN/Money, http://techland.blogs.fortune.cnn.com/2008/02/22/google-co-founder-takes-shot-at-microsofts-bid-for-yahoo/, posted February 22, 2008.
10. Stephanie Clifford, "Google Learns Lessons in the Ways of Washington," *New York Times*, October 19, 2008.

Chapter 6: A Heartbreaking IPO of Staggering Genius

1. Elisa Martinuzzi, "Google IPO Estimates Company Value at More Than $15 Billion," Bloomberg News, October 25, 2003.
2. *Seattle Post-Intelligencer*, August 3, 2004.
3. *BusinessWeek*, August 9, 2004.
4. Bill Mann, The Motley Fool, April 30, 2004, http://www.fool.com/news/take/2004/take040430.htm.
5. Paul R. La Monica, CNN/Money, August 12, 2004, http://money.cnn.com/2004/08/11/technology/techinvestor/lamonica/index.htm.
6. John Shinal, "Lifting the Google Lid: Leaders of WR Hambrecht Can Finally Talk About IPO," *San Francisco Chronicle*, September 15, 2004.
7. Kevin J. Delaney and Robin Sidel, "How Miscalculations and Hubris Hobbled Celebrated Google IPO," *Wall Street Journal*, August 19, 2004.
8. Vandana Sinha, "Reporters Approach Google IPO with Skepticism," BusinessJournalism.org, July 28, 2004.

Chapter 8: What About Privacy?

1. Lashinsky, "Can Google Three-peat?"

Chapter 9: The Ruthless Librarians

1. Eric Schmidt, "Books of Revelation," *Wall Street Journal*, October 18, 2005.
2. Motoko Rich, "Google Hopes to Open a Trove of Little-Seen Books," *New York Times*, January 4, 2009.

Chapter 10: The Google Cloud

1. You can watch the speech at http://www.youtube.com/watch?v=2FSE3TNFkJQ.

Notes

Chapter 11: Google, the Telephone Company?

1. Arshad Mohammed and Sara Kehaulani Goo, "Google Is a Tourist in D.C., Brin Finds," *Washington Post*, June 7, 2006.
2. Ibid.

Chapter 12: Thinking Beyond Search

1. Watch a video of their presentation at http://www.google.com/virgle/pioneer.html.

Afterword: Google: The New Microsoft

1. "List of acquisitions by Google," Wikipedia, http://en.wikipedia.org/wiki/List_of_acquisitions_by_Google.
2. http://googleblog.blogspot.com/2010/02/think-big-with-gig-our-experimental.html.

Index

Index

Index

Index

Index